FIRST GARDEN

##### HOW TO GET STARTED IN

# Rocky Mountain Gardening

∎

## Rob Proctor

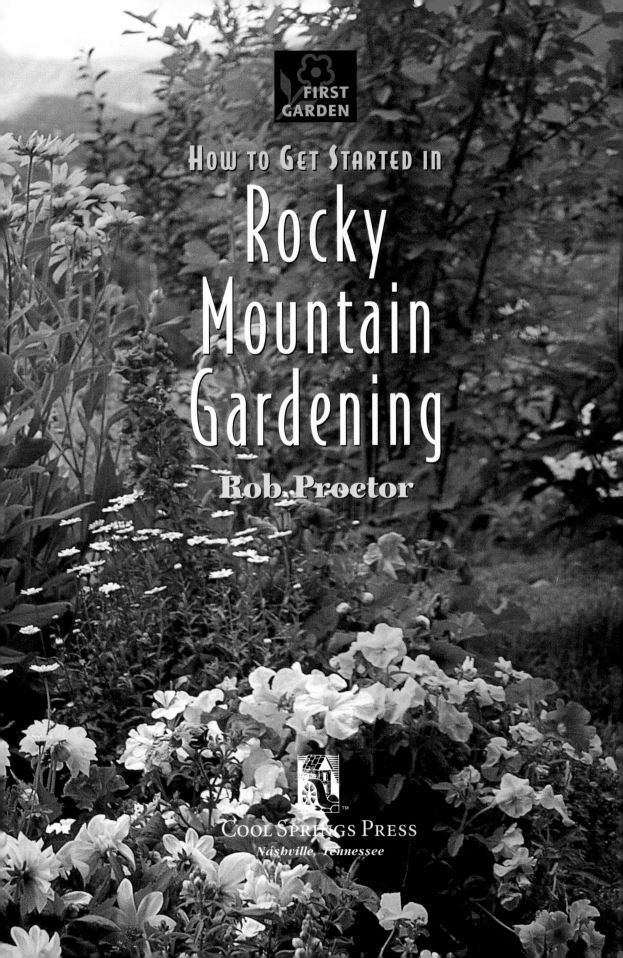

FIRST
GARDEN

## How to Get Started in

# Rocky Mountain Gardening

### Rob Proctor

Cool Springs Press
Nashville, Tennessee

Published by Cool Springs Press,
a Division of Thomas Nelson, Inc.,
P. O. Box 141000, Nashville, Tennessee 37214.

Library of Congress Cataloging-in-Publication Data
Proctor, Rob.
   How to get started in Rocky Mountain gardening / Rob Proctor.
      p. cm. — (First garden)
   Includes bibliographical references and index.
   ISBN 1-59186-158-6
   1.  Gardening--Rocky Mountains Region. 2.  Plants, Ornamental—Rocky Mountains Region.  I. Title. II. Series.
   SB453.2.R63P76 2005
   635.9'0978--dc22

                                                                    2005000213

Printed in the United States of America
10 9 8 7 6 5 4 3 2 1

Book Development & Project Management: Marlene Blessing, Marlene Blessing Editorial
Copyediting: Melanie Stafford
Design & Formatting: Constance Bollen, cb graphics
First Garden Series Consultant: Darrell Trout
Map: Bill Kersey, Kersey Graphics

**FRONT COVER: Images clockwise from upper left are sweet peas, coreopsis, variegated yucca with lamb's ears, and clematis. Photographs copyright © Rob Proctor.**

**BACK COVER: A rustic garden path in a naturalistic Rocky Mountain garden. Photograph copyright © Rob Proctor.**

---

Cool Springs Press books may be purchased in bulk
for educational, business, fundraising, or sales promotional use.
For information, please email SpecialMarkets@ThomasNelson.com.

Visit the Thomas Nelson Web site at www.ThomasNelson.com
and the Cool Springs Press Web site at www.coolspringspress.net.

*For Jeff Joyce,*

*a good gardener*

*and a great friend*

Blue flax (*Linum perenne*) with pink poppies and yellow yarrow.

# ACKNOWLEDGMENTS

Many thanks to all the gardeners
whose wonderful creations appear in my photographs:

Laura and Tim Spear
Susan Yetter
Marcia Tatroe
Mary Ellen Tonsing
Reed Johnson
Naomi and Ed Neiman
Barbara DeVoe
Angela Foster
Laurie McBride
Mary Ellen Keskimaki
Norma Hazen
Linda Heller
Rosie Catmur
Susan Lohr
Barbara and Bill Pasic
Gloria and Dan Rios
Bea Taplin
Joy and Bill Miller
Betty Ford Alpine Gardens
Blue Lake Ranch
Denver Botanic Gardens

Special thanks to David Macke for his computer expertise, my lovely and talented editor, Marlene Blessing, and the equally lovely and talented designer, Constance Bollen. I'm also grateful to Cool Springs Press for having the wisdom to understand that all gardening is regional and the foresight to initiate a gardening series—First Garden—that should introduce many first-time gardeners to the delights of successful gardening within their unique regions of the country.

## FIRST GARDEN

**ROCKY MOUNTAIN GARDENING**

'May Night' meadow sage (*Salvia nemorosa* 'May Night')

# For First-Time Gardeners Everywhere

No matter what part of the country you live in, it is possible to create a vibrant garden that adds beauty to your home and to your *life*. The First Garden series of books are meant for anyone who is just beginning to create his or her first garden. To someone who is new to gardening, a successful, thriving garden may seem like a feat to which only professionals and those with green thumbs can aspire. However, with a clear introduction to the basics—understanding your region (climate, soil, and topography); knowing the plants that grow best in your region; applying good design principles; and learning how to maintain and boost your garden's performance—you will quickly be able to start a garden. And do so with confidence! Before you know it, you may be sharing your garden dos and don'ts with your neighbor across the way.

In Section One of the book, you'll find easy-to-understand guidance to help you master the basics. As you read through this general introduction to gardening, written by nationally recognized garden expert Rob Proctor, you'll see photographs that aren't necessarily specific to your region. These are used to illustrate a design principle, technique, planting combination, or other important concept. Don't worry that your region has been forgotten! The entire final portion of the book, Section Two, is exclusively devoted to gardening specifics for your home turf. In addition to learning such things as how to improve your soil, when to plant bulbs, how to prune a tree or bush, and what kind of troubleshooting you may need to do, you'll also get a complete list of 50 sure-fire plants for your garden. Our regional garden experts have carefully selected these plants to enable you to have the best start possible as you begin what we hope will become a lifetime activity for you.

Like most pursuits, gardening takes time and patience to master. The First Garden books are designed to give you a reliable, can't-miss start. In addition to learning how to grow plants in your region, you will discover the process of turning your landscape into a beautiful, nurturing extension of your home. Even if you are beginning with only a few containers of plants on your deck or patio, you'll soon find that gardening rewards you with colors and scents that make your environment infinitely more satisfying.

With this book as your portable "garden expert," you can begin a great new adventure, knowing that you have friendly, clear advice that will keep you on the garden path. Most of all, we want to welcome you to gardening!

## The Editors at Cool Springs Press

# USDA Cold Hardiness Zone Map

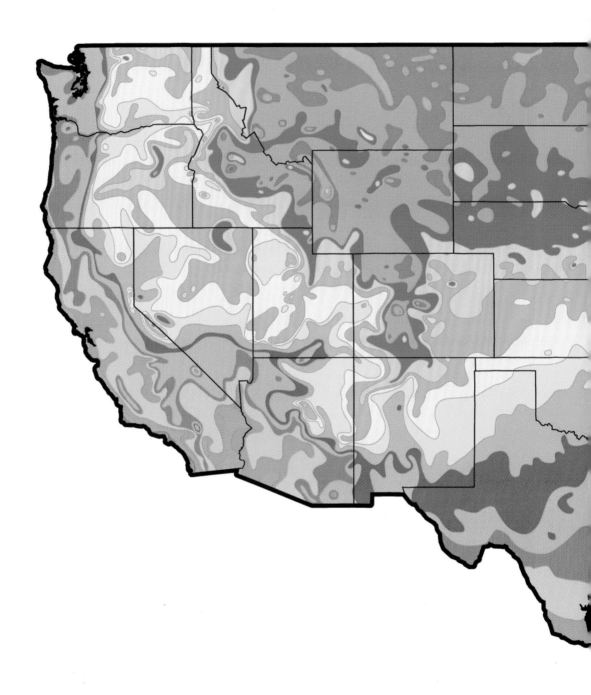

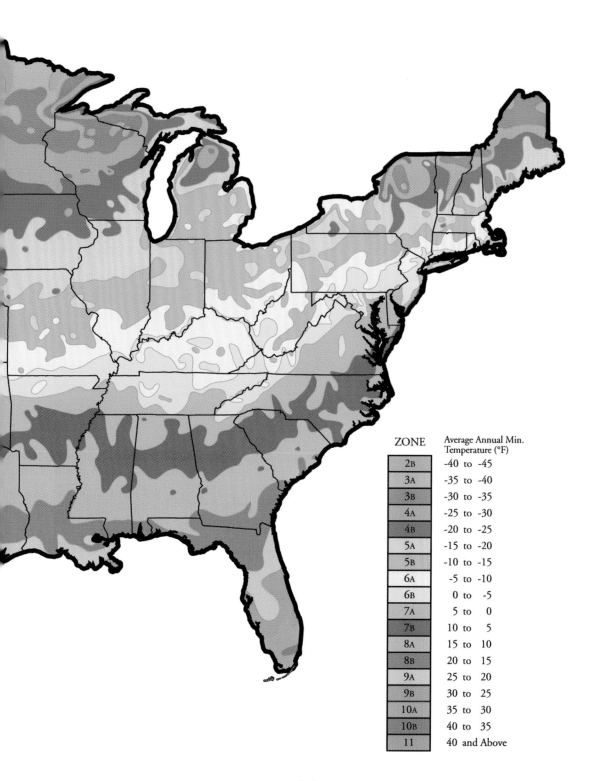

| ZONE | Average Annual Min. Temperature (°F) | |
|---|---|---|
| 2B | -40 to -45 | |
| 3A | -35 to -40 | |
| 3B | -30 to -35 | |
| 4A | -25 to -30 | |
| 4B | -20 to -25 | |
| 5A | -15 to -20 | |
| 5B | -10 to -15 | |
| 6A | -5 to -10 | |
| 6B | 0 to -5 | |
| 7A | 5 to 0 | |
| 7B | 10 to 5 | |
| 8A | 15 to 10 | |
| 8B | 20 to 15 | |
| 9A | 25 to 20 | |
| 9B | 30 to 25 | |
| 10A | 35 to 30 | |
| 10B | 40 to 35 | |
| 11 | 40 and Above | |

# Section 1

The fine textures of pine, grasses and Russian sage contrast beautifully
with purple coneflowers and yellow daylilies and daisies.

# Your First Garden

**Y**our first garden is unique. It might start as a blank canvas at a newly built house, without so much as a blade of grass. Or it could be an established landscape that you wish to make your own. Your approach will depend on your scenario. Your first garden might not even include land at the moment; perhaps, if you're an urban dweller, you've decided to garden on a rooftop or balcony.

Making a new garden is complex, intimidating, engrossing, and thrilling. It's all about color, design, and placement. Our visions dance before our eyes like sugar plum fairies. We're capable once again of that magic we used to know as children. My friend Wendy just started her first garden, and I helped her with some planning and took her shopping for plants. We filled her SUV and she rushed home to plant. She called me to say she was "enthralled in the madness" and some of our initial planning went out the window as her creative juices flowed. Good for her!

It would be rare if a garden turned out exactly as planned. However, countless TV makeover shows lead us to believe that this can happen. We see the plan, then some fast-motion digging and planting, then the finished project and the dazed surprise of the happy homeowner. This

---

**Visions spring to life in the form of satiny Iceland poppies, coral bells, and tiny 'Zing Rose' dianthus**

**Lush and romantic, this garden features roses scrambling onto a wagon wheel, coral Jupiter's beard, spikes of fireweed, and a pink skirt of Mexican evening primrose.**

all happens in the course of several days, boiled down to less than a 30-minute show. But then what? What happens to the new garden afterward?

Don't get me wrong. I like these shows and often get good design ideas from them. But without a follow-up, we don't have any idea what became of the transformation we've just witnessed. Did the owner water enough? Too much? Did the plants get enough sun? Did those vines cover the new trellis that hides that ugly garage wall? Did the perennials fill in like a soft carpet around the new pond? Or did bindweed and thistle sprout everywhere, choke out the new plants, and return the area to its former dilapidated, dismal state?

My own first garden was poorly planned, badly designed, chock-full of mistakes—and absolutely wonderful. Filled with boundless enthusiasm and unwarranted confidence from growing up in a gardening family, I blundered my way within a few years to creating a garden that was the subject of glamorous layouts in three magazines. In the process, I devoured hundreds of gardening books, subscribed to every horticultural magazine and newsletter I could find, visited every public and private garden I could, and lost twenty pounds.

I planted, transplanted, divided, amended, pruned, mulched, whacked, hacked, hoed, pinched, seeded, and fertilized until my thumb turned green. Making your first garden can be one of the most stimulating and creative experiences of your life. It might also be frustrating, confusing, and occasionally heartbreaking. It all depends on how you do it. You can take small steps or giant leaps. I'm a leaper myself, but I appreciate the cautious, practical approach, of which I'm incapable. The kind of people who plan meticulously might need a big sketch pad and several notebooks (you're probably mentally planning a shopping trip for this purpose at exactly 4:45 P.M. tomorrow afternoon). And it wouldn't hurt to construct a storyboard (borrow the bulletin board from your kid's room) of pictures and articles clipped from magazines, photos from friends' and public gardens, and even key words you want to remember as overriding themes. "Romantic," "lush," "bountiful," and "low-maintenance" don't go in the same sentence, by the way. But we'll talk about realistic maintenance later.

> My own first garden was poorly planned, badly designed, chock-full of mistakes— and absolutely wonderful.

Your notebooks can start to fill with color swatches; plant "wish lists"; clippings from the paper; brochures from fence, irrigation, and patio furniture companies; and preliminary budget figures. This might sound a bit like decorating a living room (and indeed your garden will be a "living" room), but there's a difference. With an indoor space you actually reach a point where it's considered finished. With a garden—as an evolving place—it's never completely finished, just done "for now." A garden that doesn't change is not only impossible, but I guarantee you would find it boring.

## ■ Discovering Your Inner Gardener

When you begin to garden, there are so many considerations it's tough to know where to start. So let's start with you. Do you like gardening work? That means watering, fertilizing, digging, planting, pruning, and all that? Not to mention the dreaded "W" word—weeding. Unlike tennis or ballet, gardening doesn't require any particular talents or physical attributes such as grace or brute strength. It just takes industriousness. People who like to keep house or fix cars, for example, may make fine gardeners, because the plans of attack to get the job done are similar.

Gardening is the number-one pastime in our country. Perhaps not everyone practices it to a refined degree, but this does mean that, in general, we enjoy the pleasures of working in the soil and raising flowers and vegetables. Your garden is what you make it. You'll be surprised how quickly you'll pick up the knowledge and skills to make yours beautiful and productive. Gardening is part art and part science, so there's room for everybody—right- or left-brainers— to get into the act. A friend of mine once called gardening the "slowest of the performing arts." You're the director and the plants you grow are the stars and supporting players.

As the director of your horticultural extravaganza (as well as the set designer, head writer, and entire technical crew), start with your vision. Some people might begin with a low-budget home movie, and others envision an epic blockbuster. Our inspirations come from many sources— childhood memories, books and magazines, and travels. And since I've drawn an analogy to the movies, let's acknowledge that many of us find inspiration on the silver screen as well. Sometimes

I feel my garden resembles the one in *The Secret Garden*. Before the children cleaned it up. (By the way, those were remarkably skilled kids, outperforming a crew of at least 20 landscapers.)

# ■ Blueprints for the Garden

As you plan your garden and its "rooms," take a look at what you've got—at ground level and below. City and suburban dwellers often live in a house that sits on a square, flat lot. Even a rooftop or balcony gardener usually deals with a level rectangular space. On the other hand, perhaps you live amidst hills, valleys, embankments, or even streams or ponds on your property. Your nearest neighbor may be feet or miles away.

It's probably time to clarify the difference between a landscape and a garden. Although the two are connected, there are some differences. A landscape applies to everything on the property, but most specifically trees, shrubs, and hardscape (walkways, walls, driveways, decks, patios). A landscape may include "garden areas" as a part of its overall scheme. The traditional American landscape typically features a lot of lawn, "foundation plantings" of shrubs that hug the house, and various trees placed for shade. It's a nice, familiar picture, perhaps with a strip of geraniums or petunias bordering the walk. Or maybe there's a flowerbed skirting the row of junipers or yews lined up under the eaves of the house.

The footprint of your house, any outbuildings, and adjacent buildings define your site. One way or the other, you may wish to make a blueprint of your property to draw and dream upon. It doesn't need to be exactly to scale (or even blue). I wouldn't even recommend doing much detailed planning on it since one-dimensional blueprints rarely translate into beautiful three-dimensional gardens. Just use it to familiarize yourself with all the features of your existing site (or lack of them) and for the placement of present and future walkways, driveways, patios, walls, trees, and specific garden areas or features. These could be things such as herb, cutting, or vegetable gardens as well as borders, ponds, play areas, and so forth. I often sketch on a legal pad to help me plan or revamp an area. (I once designed a friend's garden on a cocktail napkin, but that's another story that taught me I need a bigger piece of paper.)

If you picture creating a garden that is more unique, you won't need to exclude any of these traditional elements. Instead, you'll treat them somewhat differently and focus more directly on flowers and vegetables and their relationships to everything else on the property. In this scenario, there's a nearly constant, hands-on relationship between you and the plants, far beyond a weekly mowing or annual hedge trimming. If you really like plants, you can transform any static landscape into an active garden.

# ■ About Soil

What color is your thumb? People who meet me often feel obliged to apologize for their black thumbs. "I kill everything," they tell me. There's no such thing as a black thumb. Everybody can garden. Plants—like pets—need water, food, a suitable place to live, and occasional grooming. Green thumbs aren't born, they're made. The origin of the term stems from the fact that gardeners put excessive wear and tear on their thumbs and forefingers. As they pinch petunias or pull pigweed, the green sap stains eventually become engrained for most of the gardening season. My thumb's not a classic green but more of a dirty olive tone. Let's not mention my knuckles and nails, which are accented by various cuts, scrapes, and punctures.

You don't need to ruin your hands. Sensible glove-wearing gardeners still deserve the title green thumb. You can earn it, too. Learn the basics and build on those, just the way you'd approach any new pastime such as cooking, tennis, sewing, or carpentry.

Okay, former black thumbs: get started. Dig a spadeful of soil. (If you're a rooftop or balcony gardener, skip this and go buy some potting soil.) Squeeze a handful. Does it stick together into a mud ball? You have clay. That's most of us. If the ball of soil falls apart, you've got sand. It's an easier soil to dig, but dries out more quickly. If you're extremely lucky, you're blessed with rich, black "Iowa cornfield" soil that gardeners crave (in which case you're probably reading this in Iowa). Don't worry. Both clay and sandy soil can be amended to grow some traditional plants. On the other hand, a good many plants are so adaptable that they'll grow well in almost any kind of soil.

Once you've done some experimenting, you can decide what—if anything—you want to do to your soil. I actually don't amend soil, but grow what wants to grow in that soil. I've often read or seen experts who recommend a soil test. I've never done one. I wouldn't have a clue what it meant if I had 100 parts magnesium

**Green thumbs aren't born, they're made.**

**A garden planted in unimproved clay soil, rarely irrigated, supports many drought-tolerant perennials including varieties of penstemons and bright Jupiter's beard.**

per million. Unless you suspect that your soil has an actual problem (such as being missing after the builders finished the house) or has some sort of contamination, I can't imagine the value of a test unless you want to grow rare alpine plants from Switzerland. Even if your soil has been pounded and pulverized by heavy equipment, you don't need a soil test to tell you it's been compacted and that with just a little more pressure will turn into diamonds. Most people have the kind of soil that everybody else in their neighborhood has. What's growing there? Does it look healthy? If the trees are dying and lawns are sickly, don't get a soil test—call the Environmental Protection Agency.

Your soil will actually teach you as you go along what it's capable of doing. It may not support absolutely every type of plant you might want to grow (I'll never have blueberries), but odds are it has plenty of potential. For extreme sand or clay, you may decide to amend or alter your soil or bring in topsoil for plants with specific needs (I would need to create an acidic bog to grow blueberries). But first explore what your soil can do before you begin a wholesale radical makeover that will forever alter its composition.

Don't just start adding ingredients willy-nilly. Many books often recommend adding lime to the soil as a matter of course. The assumption is that most plants do best if grown in a soil that is about neutral on the pH scale. This advice may be all well and good in Cleveland or Boston where the soil pH is on the acid side, for the lime would reduce the acidity. But for gardeners in the West, which generally has an alkaline soil, the lime would be a waste of time, like giving "The Rock" a gym membership for his birthday. The point is to be familiar with your soil type and composition, but don't stress about it.

# ■ Weather and Gardening Zones

Before you start thinking about planting, determine in which climate zone you live. The U.S. Department of Agriculture (USDA) issues a detailed map, found at the front of this book, that illustrates these zones throughout the country. Based primarily on average minimum temperatures, the map helps you determine which plants will survive in your area. Almost all the plants you buy will be rated as to the zones where they are hardy, meaning where they'll survive an average winter. Most nurseries in your region only carry plants that are appropriate to it. But if you purchase plants online or by mail, you should be aware of your zone so you don't end up planting a tropical palm in Minnesota.

Many gardeners expand their options by clever gardening known as "zone denial."

## IN THE ZONE

The USDA climate zone map is a good aid in helping you decide what to grow, but it has its limitations. For example, it doesn't take into account rainfall, humidity, and, most importantly, high temperatures. These factors also affect plant survival. You'll find that Chicago, Denver, and Hartford are all categorized as zone 5, but their actual growing conditions vary considerably. Rainfall, humidity, and summer heat—as well as soil type—may play as great a role in plant performance as winter low temperatures. Southern gardeners sometimes find that plants considered hardy for their zone won't thrive in their summer heat or need a colder winter dormancy than southern climes provide. Tulips are a case in point. It all sounds terribly complicated, but as you visit local nurseries and gardens, you'll get the hang of it. You'll soon start to get a grasp of what wants to grow in your area.

# MICROCLIMATES

Adhering to the zone designations may help you play it safe, but many gardeners expand their options by clever gardening known as "zone denial." After all, plants can't read. If they receive the conditions that allow them to thrive, they will. This is where knowing your garden site intimately is vital. Throughout it there are "microclimates," little pockets formed by topography, fences, trees, and walls. Your house offers the most differentiations. Southern and western exposures are usually hotter and sunnier; northern and eastern exposures, cooler and shadier. The placement of trees can moderate or enhance these conditions.

A hill or outcropping may afford at least two distinct microclimates in much the same way as your house does. Lower areas tend to be cooler and, because cold air sinks, often freeze earlier than higher ground, as well as collecting and holding moisture. Knowing this helps you to position plants that prefer either well-drained soil (on a slope) or moist soil (in a hog wallow). Both air and water drain in the same manner on a large scale. Cold air often "flows" along streams and rivers, making low-lying areas "frost pockets" and higher ground "banana belts." If you're in a low-lying area, there's not much you can do about this, of course, except to be more cautious about setting out tender plants in spring or protecting them in the fall. If you're on a hilltop, you can just feel smug. But hilltops may get fierce winds (in gardening, there's a plus and minus to every condition). Knowing the direction of the prevailing wind helps prevent mistakes as well; otherwise you may be staking your delphiniums with rebar.

Paving and foundations, as well as rocks and rock outcrops also affect plant performance, either for better or worse, depending on the plant. Some plants revel in the extra heat from driveways, walkways, and foundations, and others can't stand baking. Many plants also like to get their roots beneath rocks and paving not only because of the extra heat, but because the mass of the stone moderates the surrounding temperatures by virtue of its slow heating and cooling. Rock gardeners exploit these possibilities to the max, with every nook and cranny offering a potential microclimate for a special plant.

Wherever you live, you can create a beautiful garden. Gardeners often envy others who live in different climates, usually because of particular plants that grow beautifully in that environment. By all means, experiment to see if you can achieve similar results. But don't get hung up on a certain flower that has little intention of performing for you. Yes, I've made attempts to grow azaleas and rhododendrons that I admire in friends' gardens in Virginia. And failed. So I'm content to visit them in spring and enjoy their good fortune. They come to see me, too, to admire western specialties that their gardens can't accommodate successfully, like prickly poppies and penstemons.

Although we often equate an abundance of moisture with successful gardening, it's only because the spectacular gardens in rainy regions get most of the good press. Lovely, original gardens are found within every region of our country. They are filled with the plants that want to grow there. Some may be native wildflowers, and others may originate in areas around the

**A rock-terraced slope provides good drainage and extra heat for purple verbena, agave, and ice plants, with a backdrop of golden black-eyed Susans.**

world with similar climate and soil. Fortunately for all of us, there's an enormous pool of plants that offer amazing abilities to adapt to a wide spectrum of conditions. Like our country itself, your new garden is likely to become a melting pot of flowers and styles from many lands— with your very own personal stamp.

# ■ Plant Names: Why Latin?

There's no escaping it. You need a little Latin—not much, but a little. Every living thing, animal and plant, is classified scientifically using a system that speaks Latin. To keep the millions of distinct forms of life in some sort of reasonable order, they all have a scientific name, much like our first and last names. It avoids duplication. If you looked in the phone book under Mary Jones or Bob Smith, you understand how confusing it could get if we just called plants "bluebell" or "daisy."

Most people know more scientific plant names than they think. Even non-gardeners are familiar with *chrysanthemum, geranium, lobelia, dahlia, crocus, phlox, gardenia, verbena, begonia,* and *petunia.* Others aren't much of a stretch, such as *rosa* for rose, *lilium* for lily, *tulipa* for tulip, or *hyacinthus* for hyacinth.

Within any genus of plants or animals there are individual species. Let's start with people. We all belong to the genus *Homo,* meaning human. And our species is *sapiens,* meaning wise or intelligent. We belong to the classification "intelligent human." We don't need to draw this distinction very often since the rest of the members of our genus are extinct. *Homo erectus* was "standing man," who apparently could walk upright but wasn't known for his brain. The traits of particular plants are often noted in their species name, called the specific epitaph, such as their color, habit, size, leaf shape, their resemblance to something else, what habitat they grow in, their country or region of origin, or something like that. They don't always make a whole lot of sense. Sometimes they honor a botanist who first discovered them or somebody to whom the discoverer wanted to suck up. After all, who wouldn't want a plant named for them? Most plants were named hundreds of years ago, although new discoveries occasionally crop up in rain forests.

When plant breeders get involved, plants acquire yet another name. Say that you, as a plant breeder, cross two different species to create a brand-new offspring with distinctly different characteristics from the two parents. Or say that, as a sharp-eyed gardener or nursery owner, you spot an unusual variation in an otherwise uniform batch of plants. What do you do? Name it, of course, for your wife, husband, mother, daughter, or a celebrity you admire. Or if you're more creative, you go for something more lyrical or amusing. That's why we have *Anemone* x *hybrida* 'Honorine Jobert' (named for the guy's daughter), the hybrid tea rose 'Dolly Parton' (a voluptuous flower), and the self-descriptive petunia 'Purple Wave' (the color really flows). I've always hoped to create a new color of the trailing annual *Bacopa* and call it 'Cabana'. The gardening world is waiting. . . .

**Penstemon fanciers need to know the scientific names of pink *Penstemon palmeri* and purple *P. strictus.***

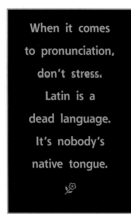

**When it comes to pronunciation, don't stress. Latin is a dead language. It's nobody's native tongue.**

As for the scientific names, we don't use them very much except for perennials. Not too many people say *quercus* instead of oak or *curcubita* instead of squash (unless they're really, really snobbish). Whenever a common name will do, use it. Most gardeners—in my opinion—should just talk about daylilies, Russian sage, and yarrow without trying to tie their tongues around *hemerocallis, perovskia,* or *achillea*. But in some cases, especially when you're talking about a genus with a whole bunch of species, and you need to get specific about which one, the only way is to use Latin. There are hundreds of varieties of *penstemon*, for example. These lovely western wildflowers, commonly called beardtongue (yuck), range from tall scarlet *Penstemon barbatus* to mat-forming blue *Penstemon virens*. Then there's pretty orange *P. pinifolius*, lovely pink *P. palmeri*, and wispy white *P. ambiguas*. If you get into penstemons, you gotta speak the lingo.

When it comes to pronunciation, don't stress. Latin is a dead language. It's nobody's native tongue. Do your best with this cumbersome old language. And if someone dares to correct your pronunciation of a name, just stare him or her down coolly and say, "Oh, that's the way I used to say it." This implies that you have been hanging out with more knowledgeable gardeners than they have and you must obviously be right.

Sort out the easy mispronunciations before you go to the nursery so you don't have them snickering behind your back. *Cotoneaster* is "ka-tone-ee-aster" not "cotton Easter." I'd say flowering tobacco for *nicotiana*, but if you must, pronounce it "ni-coh-she-anna" not "nikko-teen-a." Avoid *aquilegia* ("ah-qui-lee-ja" not "a-quill-a-gee-a"), and just say columbine instead.

# ■ Plant Types

## TREES: GARDEN ELDERS

All this talk of sites, soils, and climates brings us to the basic business of knowing and growing plants. Plants have evolved to fill niches created by geography and topography. Trees tower above everything (sort of like carnivores on the food chain). They're tough and long-lived. Any tree planted today will, with care, likely outlive any of us, so its placement is the most critical of any plant you put in the soil. Trees need space. With their specific needs varying by species, they need enough room between them and your house, each other, power lines, and features like that. In most cities, the office of forestry offers guidelines and regulations on tree planting. Street trees especially must be placed so as to not block sight lines at intersections or to interfere with power lines and street lights. If you get it wrong, some city employee will probably pay you a visit. Some kinds and types of trees are even forbidden because they are brittle and are prone to breaking under snow and ice or from wind, which endangers cars and passersby. Multistemmed trees such as redbuds or dogwoods are often prohibited for planting along streets since they can block the views at intersections. Most drivers can see around a single trunk tree adequately, but a big mass of foliage is dangerous.

**Breaks in the canopy of trees allows beds of perennials and ornamental grasses
to flourish in this well-conceived plan.**

Trees differ in many ways. Evergreens hold their leaves (called needles if the tree is a spruce, pine, fir, or cypress) throughout the year, while deciduous trees drop their leaves in fall and grow new ones in spring. In frost-free climates, some trees hold their leaves throughout the year, while others still go through a seasonal renewal. At least two kinds of "evergreen" tree, the larch and bald cypress, go dormant in fall and drop their needles. There's an infamous tale in my city of a park maintenance crew who, thinking that it had died, cut down a prized bald cypress that was just in the bald phase of its normal cycle.

All trees flower. Some do it in spectacular fashion, while others are barely noticed except by allergy sufferers. Bees and other insects usually pollinate trees with big, showy, and scented flowers, such as fruit trees. Most other trees rely on the wind to blow about their massive amounts of pollen, which is precisely why spring can be so miserable for some of us.

Most trees have a single main trunk, and most deciduous trees create an interlocking canopy of branches. Trunks of every tree should always be respected and protected. While appearing to be the strongest part of the tree, the trunk is also the most vulnerable. Just beneath the bark is the lifeline of the tree, called the cambium layer, the vascular system that supports the tree the way our veins and arteries support us. When bark is damaged, that damage is usually irreversible, and the limbs on that side of the tree will often die. Even something as insignificant as a weed whacker can damage or kill a tree.

Tree roots need respect and protection, too. Compaction of the soil above the roots is to be avoided as this suffocates them and inhibits their ability to absorb water. The roots that do most of the work of searching for food and water, called feeder roots, are usually at and beyond the shady circle cast by the tree at high noon. This is called the drip line, because rain splashes from leaf to leaf, keeping the area directly beneath relatively dry. Remember that it doesn't do much good to water a tree right at the trunk since its feeder roots are many feet away.

## WOODY PLANTS: SPACE AND CARE

Trees are durable because they're made of wood. This is either patently obvious or extremely profound, but I thought it needed to be said. Other woody plants—call them shrubs or bushes, it doesn't matter—are structured like trees. They can also be deciduous or evergreen, but their main similarity is their strong, woody constitution. All the considerations you give to a tree in placement and care apply to shrubs. One of the chronic mistakes that plague American gardeners is to crowd shrubs and not give them enough room to develop. This leads to much whacking and hacking, resulting in distorted, weird-looking bushes, often represented by the classic "light bulb" trim job. I know you've seen it. You've probably also driven past houses that have almost completely disappeared behind rampaging junipers whose growth habits the owners underestimated. There's a hilarious example in my neighborhood where the people neglected to read the tags when they planted cone-shaped junipers in front of their picture windows. Eventually, the view disappeared as the trees grew higher than the house. The owners then decided to trim all the branches below the roofline, leaving thick bare trunks with little "Christmas trees" perched upon them. I chuckle every time I drive by, but there's a lesson in that for all of us.

Most shrubs we grow in our gardens are either selected for their evergreen nature (often for winter interest) or for their flowers. A few, such as holly, are grown primarily for their handsome berries. Almost all flowering shrubs bloom on "old" wood, meaning only branches a year or more old will produce flowers. Keep in mind that if you do prune or trim (shrubs usually need much less grooming than we think), it should be done only right after they've finished blooming. Otherwise you'll be cutting off your next years' display.

## ROSES: TENDER OR TOUGH

Roses are certainly the most popular of the shrubs. Novice gardeners want to grow them in the worst way. First-time rose growers envision huge bouquets of long-stemmed tea roses on their dining room tables. It's a nice dream, but those roses you received on Valentine's Day were greenhouse grown in supporting cages to keep their stems straight and long. And the bushes never experienced arctic winters or Saharan heat. Yours probably will.

Let's get realistic about roses. You'll have some for cutting, but don't get any ideas about opening your own flower shop. Wherever you garden, you can successfully grow hundreds of varieties of roses. Just don't get hung up on the hybrid teas at the beginning. Just as rewarding are the old-fashioned shrub roses, climbers, floribundas, and the so-called landscape roses and carpet roses. Most thrive with a minimum of care and some are even drought tolerant.

Shrub roses say romance in the garden. With their graceful, arching canes laden with sweet blooms, they conjure nostalgic visions of castles and cottages. Superb performers, they seldom, if ever, suffer from pests or diseases beyond an aphid or two (easily dispatched with a soapy spray). Widely grown across much of the nation are the classic early bloomers such as 'Persian

Yellow', 'Austrian Copper', and 'Harrison's Yellow'. The red-leaf rose, *Rosa glauca*, takes the prize as the most adaptable shrub rose. It will thrive in conditions from sun to part shade, clay to sand, and wet to dry. Pretty little single pink flowers grace the unusual leaves, blue-gray on top with maroon red underneath.

These large shrub roses can often be found in older neighborhoods where they put on spectacular early displays. Young shrub roses are like gawky teenagers, irregular and awkward looking. Give them space and time to fulfill their promise. Some people avoid planting these classics because they bloom only once each season. That's unfair. After all, I've never heard anyone complain because his or her lilacs, tulips, or lilies bloom only once a year.

Some shrub roses do bloom persistently, even in heat. The *rugosa* hybrids are simply wonderful. If I had to choose just one, it would be 'Therese Bugnet' (pronounced "boon-yay"). On bushes 4' by 5', its glossy green foliage supports full, pink flowers with the perfect "old rose" perfume. I'm also entranced by 'Golden Wings', an upright shrub type that grows to 4' or 5' tall. Its huge, single amber yellow flowers are accented by orange stamens and carry a soft fragrance. For an arbor or trellis, the classic ruby red 'Blaze' can't be beat, while pale pink 'New Dawn' is the stuff of fairy tales. Speaking of which, 'The Fairy' is a dainty but tough little shrub about 3' by 3' with nonstop clusters of satin pink blooms. It's beautiful with lavender or catmint as a "skirt" (most roses are lovely coupled with these plants). All these roses grow well in most regions, but there are certainly regional favorites that you can visit at local municipal gardens. Look

> **Wherever you garden, you can successfully grow hundreds of varieties of roses.**

**Adobe-toned yarrow and a flurry of snow daisies enhance the much-admired classic hybrid tea rose 'Peace.'**

Vines are really just shrubs with a posture problem.

for ones that demonstrate unusual vigor and clean, disease-free leaves. Also keep in mind how much room you want to devote to each bush. Can you accommodate the big boys, or are you best with the little guys?

Other compact varieties that perform tirelessly are the Meidiland series in white, coral, reds, and pinks. Easy and prolific, their single or double flowers fit in effortlessly with perennials such as meadow sage, pincushion flowers, catmints, snow daisies, and yarrow. Most roses—to my mind—look their best planted informally rather than regimented in rows. Hybrid tea roses benefit enormously when surrounded by casual companions that enhance their charms and disguise their weaknesses. To keep the advice short and sweet: plant roses in sun, keep them evenly moist, feed regularly, and prune in spring. I'm fond of a number of hybrid tea roses, but my favorite is the elegant cream and pink 'Peace'. This classic rose, bred in France just before World War II, survived because its breeder shipped a single cutting to a friend in America just before the Nazis invaded. The rest of the roses were destroyed, but 'Peace' endured. Just one of its flowers, floating in a bowl, is all any rose lover needs.

## VINES: BEAUTIFUL CLIMBERS

Vines are really just shrubs with a posture problem. They've found a special niche in nature where they rely on their neighbors for support. The ultimate in social climbers, they cling and twine their way to ever-greater heights. Since they are lovely, we forgive them and give them fences, arbors, and trellises on which to grow and flower. Some enchant us with their flowers—clematis, honeysuckle, and wisteria—and others with their foliage—ivy and Virginia creeper. Grapes mean jelly, juice, and wine, and hops are a vital ingredient in beer. I've never made homemade wine or beer, but both grapes and hops make beautiful, albeit rambunctious, additions to the garden. A few very popular vines, such as morning glories and sweet peas, grow, flower, and die in one season, which makes them annuals. We'll talk about them shortly.

**A planting of roses and perennials, including pink lupines and white valerian, is peppered with annual bread seed poppies.**

## PERENNIALS: LASTING PLEASURES

Perennial plants have a completely different strategy for survival than trees and shrubs. When cold weather hits, they retreat underground and wait out winter with their root systems. They return "perennially" each spring. Don't confuse "perennial" with "immortal," however, as some

**Annuals in concert—glowing pink 'First Love' dianthus scores with blue and white forms of mealy-cup sage.**

perennials run their course in just a few years. Others live to a very old age, such as peonies and daylilies. Since about the last quarter of the twentieth century, most Americans have based the bulk of their gardens around perennials. Just as hemlines go up and down and lapels go wide and then skinny, gardens go through periods of what's in and out. At the moment and for the foreseeable future, perennials figure prominently in most gardens. With trees and shrubs as the backdrop and structure of the garden, perennials take center stage. They're valued for their diversity, toughness, longevity, and—above all—beauty. A wonderful trend in American gardening today is to value every sort of plant and use it to best advantage. While Victorians didn't have much use for perennials, preferring showy, hothouse-raised annuals, we've come to embrace all kinds of plants regardless of their life cycles.

## ANNUALS: COLORFUL ADDITIONS

When we picture annuals, we think of those vibrant, tempting flowers bursting out of their six-packs every spring at garden centers, supermarkets, and home improvement stores. These are the plants we rely on for continuous color all summer long. Usually grown from seed, annuals germinate, grow, flower, set seed, and die in a single season. It's a short, but dazzling life cycle. What's considered an annual depends on where you live. In most northern climates, the annual section includes many tender tropical and subtropical perennials, such as geraniums, that aren't hardy below freezing. My sister in Florida has geraniums older than her ancient cat. So in this category, we're including plants with a single-season life cycle in whichever climate you garden. Your local nursery can help you sort it all out. Many gardeners in cold-winter climates move these tender perennials indoors to save them from year to year.

Most annuals come packaged in handy six-packs or four-packs, but for the impatient, many garden centers offer mature blooming annuals in quart- or gallon-size pots. These, of course, come with higher price tags, but presumably are worth it for those who want instant gratification. A number of annuals aren't very suitable for six-packs, and grow best if sown directly in the ground. You'll save money as well as expand your selection if you learn to grow plants from seed. To build your confidence, start with the easy ones like sunflowers and marigolds.

Annuals prove themselves invaluable in a new garden because they grow to full size quickly. While everything else—trees, shrubs, and perennials—put down roots for the long haul, annuals fill the gaps and encourage the new gardener. But they're much more than gap-fillers. Even as the rest of the garden takes off, leave room for the gorgeous gaiety that annuals provide. I'd never want to go through a season without the brilliant blossoms of California poppies, moss roses, larkspurs, zinnias, or salvias. Annuals truly shine in container gardens as well. As mentioned previously, several vines are annual in nature. Among the most popular are morning glories, sweet peas, hyacinth beans, sweet potato vines, canary creepers, and climbing nasturtiums, not to mention peas and pole beans.

Many annuals that find your garden to their liking may respond by sowing themselves from year to year, making a one-time investment in them a very good one indeed. These "volunteers" can be thinned and transplanted to suit you. Johnny-jump-ups, larkspurs, bachelor's buttons, sweet alyssum, and several kinds of poppy—California, Shirley, corn, and lettuce-leaf—likely will form colonies in your garden. Count yourself lucky.

The care of annuals is as diverse as the plants themselves. Some like constant attention with lots of water and fertilizer. Some prefer benign neglect. Morning glories, cosmos, and nasturtiums—if fed and watered too much—will reward you with jungle-like growth, but deny you their flowers. It's called too much of a good thing.

## BULBS: SPRING AND FALL

Bulbs take their preservation to extremes. Spring-flowering bulbs such as tulips and daffodils bide their wintertime underground, plumping themselves up with moisture. As winter retreats, the flowers of the bulb emerge. Sometimes they're a bit ahead of schedule and get caught by late freezes and snowstorms. Don't stress about your tulips, hyacinths, crocuses, daffodils, or snowdrops. They've evolved to bloom at that tricky time when winter and spring wrestle for dominance. They can withstand frost and snow (even if some flower stems snap). If they couldn't, they'd be extinct. If a heavy, wet snow threatens your tulips at the height of perfection, by all means cover them with bushel baskets, buckets, card tables, or whatever sheltering device you have handy. But these early bulbs don't need a blanket to keep them warm; they grow and flower best during the cool, sunny days of spring.

**LEFT: Fall-blooming crocus belie the season with their springlike charms, contrasted by reddening plumbago foliage. RIGHT: Late spring-blooming Dutch iris pair attractively with variegated dogwood.**

When things heat up, the spring bulbs finish their annual cycle by setting seed, soaking up the sun to provide energy for the next spring, and going through their ugly phase of unkempt, yellowing leaves. The best thing you can do is snap off their seedpods so they don't waste the energy, fertilize the plants to ensure a great display next spring, and ignore the yellowing leaves until they've turned brown. If you cut or pull off the foliage prematurely, you'll likely affect the bulb's ability to turn in a star performance next season. Live with it. By planting the bulbs farther back in beds—rather than right at the edge—emerging perennials will help camouflage the dying bulb leaves.

Summer doesn't spell the end of bulbs. Some even bloom in fall. The term bulb, by the way, refers to the enlarged roots that have evolved over time for each kind of bulbous plant. Some are categorized as true bulbs (tulips and lilies), some as corms (crocuses and gladiolus), some as rhizomes (irises), and others as tubers (dahlias). They all vary in shape and size, but they are all efficient storage containers. And the great thing is that they can sit dormant for months while they zip around the world, arriving at planting time at your neighborhood nursery. Then these hard brown chunks get buried, send out roots, plump up, and emerge above ground to grow and flower. I've always found that wondrous and wonderful.

The summer bulbs may be either hardy or tender, depending, once again, on where you garden. For most people, lilies, irises, and liatris can be treated as perennials. The rest of them— dahlias, cannas, elephant ears, caladiums, and gladiolus—must be dug after frost and their bulbs, corms, rhizomes, and tubers stored over winter.

**Startling Flanders poppies seed themselves among an easy-care collection of classic bearded iris that are cut back and divided every four or five years.**

I must warn you here about falling into a very bad habit concerning bearded iris. I adore these plants, so I feel protective toward them. Anyway, irises grow quickly, and to keep them healthy and blooming, you need to divide them every four or five years. After they flower in late spring, you dig up a clump and break up the rhizomes into pieces about six inches long with a single "fan" of leaves. You replant each fan right near the soil surface with 6" to 8" between each piece. Now here's the important part: Because the rhizome has a lot of work to do in getting its roots reestablished, you help out by cutting the fan of leaves down by half with scissors. The roots can't support all that top growth. If you follow these directions, you'll grow superb iris. However, never cut back the foliage unless you're transplanting the iris. For some odd reason, millions of Americans think they should go out after these bloom and punish their iris for a job well done by disfiguring the leaves and cutting off half of their system of making food. If I see you've done it, I'll knock on your door and give you a stern lecture. I travel extensively, so don't think you're safe just because you live in Salt Lake City or Sheboygan.

Summer- and autumn-flowering bulbs make amazing contributions to the garden and patio pots. I'm especially fond of cannas, lilies, and dahlias in big pots as exotic, colorful exclamation points on terraces and patios. Often overlooked, fall-blooming bulbs add enchantment to our gardens late in the season. Put a note in your daytimer to buy and plant them in late summer and early fall. It's worth the effort. Fall crocuses bring a touch of spring to our beds and borders even as the backdrop changes to yellow and bronze. Springing from the earth without leaves, these pretty flowers are ideally planted in concert with low-growing ground cover perennials such as thyme, partridge feather, and plumbago. Unusual in their life cycles, these bulbs send up their leaves in spring, soak up the sun, and disappear until their surprise late performance.

## HERBS: USEFUL AND BEAUTIFUL

It used to be that the only herbs most folks encountered were lavender in their soaps, some mint in their juleps, and perhaps some parsley garnishing their dinner plates. Thank goodness those days are gone. As we all hunger for a healthier, tastier diet, herbs have become invaluable in our kitchens. We find them in many facets of our lives, from the medicine cabinet to the bathtub and the linen closet. Many people classify herbs as the "useful plants," whether they're used for culinary, cosmetic, medicinal, or household purposes.

An herb garden can be a charming garden room. Alternately, herbs lend themselves to growing in borders or vegetable and cutting gardens as well as pots. One big misconception that you may have heard

> As we all hunger for a healthier, tastier diet, herbs have become invaluable in our kitchens.

**An unusual "scare camel" protects a country garden that rivals those in southern France for charm, with its casual mix of lavender, daisies, poppies and ornamental onions.**

repeated is that herbs like terrible soil and tough conditions. This, of course, depends on your soil type, but I guess it stems from the fact that many popular cooking herbs come from the Mediterranean region. Oregano, thyme, tarragon, rosemary, lavender, savory, and sage love full sun, don't need much water, and prosper in a mineral-rich, not-too-fluffed-up soil. To some people, that means poor soil; but for most of us, that's what we've got. Other herbs such as basil or ginger like organically rich, moist soil. Herbs display the same diversity as any other group of plants but, in general, are quite adaptable. Many that you wish to grow may thrive happily in a room devoted strictly to them. As you grow and experiment with this fascinating group, your kitchen and home will change forever.

## TURF: WISE CARE

One of my summer chores growing up was tending the lawn. I hated it. But I learned what it took to have a healthy lawn with minimal effort (never underestimate an adolescent who'd rather be doing something else). Fertilize and aerate in spring and fall. Dig dandelions by hand the minute they start to bloom. Water during the coolest part of the day. And water infrequently and deeply to encourage the roots to delve deeply in search of water. Roots near the surface burn up. Set the mower blade at the highest level, the better to shade the roots during hot weather.

I've stood by these early findings ever since, and I've always had healthy, resilient lawns with a minimum of crabgrass (which I also hand-dig before it goes to seed) and never an instance of mold, fungus, or the other horrors that seem to plague overwatered grass. An inch of moisture a week is not only sufficient but also advisable for a tough turf that can roll with the punches. If you get moss in parts of your lawn, consider this: perhaps nature is telling you that moss would be more suitable than turf. Some of the most beautiful "lawns" I've seen in New England were made of moss.

I've recently reached a point in my life where I am lawn-free. The recent western drought pushed me over the edge. I don't begrudge anyone else's right to enjoy their lawn for family activities and, perhaps, the pleasure of tending it. Just do it responsibly and wisely to get the most out of your work and water. Many seasoned gardeners I know have little or no lawn. It all starts by expanding the borders by a foot or two. Sometimes a gardening couple will argue about whether this is necessary (husbands tend to treasure the time spent with their lawns), but eventually the border prevails.

As you plan your new garden, you may be starting with nothing more than a lawn. Ask yourself, "Do I really want that responsibility, to maintain a lawn up to the neighborhood standard?" It's work. Flower and vegetable gardening is work, too, but a lot less monotonous, and (in my opinion) infinitely more rewarding. Limiting the size of turf areas reduces water consumption and allows you to better care for what you've got. Eventually, I'd guess, you'll be nibbling away at the edges to make more room for flowers.

## GROUND COVERS AND TURF ALTERNATIVES: ALONE OR TOGETHER

While various kinds of turf are the ultimate ground covers, a number of low-growing, low-maintenance perennials can serve much the same purpose. They're not suitable for badminton or dodgeball, but they offer a pretty alternative to the big stretch of green lawn. They're also

**A tapestry of ground covers on a rocky slope includes sedums, snow-on-the-mountain, and ice plants, punctuated by flaming Oriental poppies.**

ideal for slopes, hills, and irregular terrain that may be a challenge to mow. You can choose to plant a single ground cover, such as a moss or thyme. Or you can plant many kinds of ground covers as a tapestry of intertwining colors and textures. The best ground covers for your area will be found at your local nursery. Widely grown kinds include creeping veronica, thyme, brass button, ivy, lily turf (*Liriope*), pachysandra, lamium, vinca, wine cup, partridge feather, creeping baby's breath, mat daisy, Irish and Scottish moss, creeping phlox, hen and chicks, sedum, and ice plant. In addition, many require less water than most lawn grasses and little or no fertilization. And you never need to mow. Your world will become a quieter place.

# ■ Your Style

Never give up your vision. Style transcends climate. Almost everything is possible, budget and patience permitting. At the same time, consider the region in which you live and its natural landscape, as well as its signature plants—whether native (meaning indigenous) or not—that provide its gardening identity. After all, what's Portland without roses, Phoenix without saguaro cacti, New Orleans without bougainvillea vines, Richmond without dogwood trees, Denver without

Style transcends climate. Almost everything is possible, budget and patience permitting.

Southwestern gardeners draw on the desert and Native American cultures for inspiration, as strong architectural plants make a bold style statement.

blue spruce, or Washington, D.C., without cherry trees? The gardening heritage of your city or state may be an important factor in determining the style and contents of your garden.

The architecture of your home also figures into that determination. My modest turn-of-the-century cottage would look downright silly with a Louis XIV clipped ornamental garden, complete with formal pools and statuary. Conversely, a naturalistic meadow would appear equally out of place surrounding a stately brick Tudor home. We all borrow from other places and other times when conceiving our garden visions. Translating them into reality is what it's all about. For example, my garden is a hybrid between the classic perennial border garden and a cottage garden. Some might claim, "You can't do an English garden in Denver!" (or Kansas City or Charlotte or wherever you live). But they've disregarded the fact that any style of garden is simply that—a style. Had I planted mine with plants that thrive in England, I'd be doomed to failure. As it is, my English-themed garden has a Colorado twist, featuring flowers that survive and thrive in my dry, hot-in-summer, cold-in-winter climate. Plants don't know or care about style; they're satisfied when they get the right spot in the right garden.

# ■ Garden Rooms

Rooms organize a house. Most of us bathe in one room, cook in another, sleep, do laundry, play, read, and watch TV in others. Some rooms do double duty. Others don't do much. Unlike its namesake, for instance, the living room is often the least lived-in room in the house.

Rooms can also organize a garden (and they are really "living" rooms), even if they're not strictly for daily activities. When I'm in the garden, I'd just as soon ignore dirty dishes, piles of laundry, and the day's top stories. Time spent in a garden is unlike any other activity. Some days it's all about color and excitement. Others are about manicuring and attention to details. War is occasionally declared on weeds, while every once in awhile a day is dreamy and peaceful.

My garden is organized into several rooms. Some are for the pleasure and convenience of people, others for the specific requirements of the plants in them (shade, sun, moisture, etc.). As with the rooms of a house, these garden rooms demand care and attention. Like an interior designer who creates a room, I rarely get to use it the way it's intended. I'm more of a maid with dirty nails and knees. But that's my own fault: I've made my (garden) bed, now I must lie in it.

When friends come over, I'm forced to enjoy my garden. While I join in the conversation, music, and wine, however, I'm secretly thinking that the flowering maple over there is looking droopy and I've just got to get those bug-bitten leaves off the golden sweet potato vine. And that begonia really ought to be deadheaded. Right now! Pretty gardens do require time and the right kind of work at the right time. But perhaps the emphasis I've placed on the work involved to create one is misleading. It's not really work, after all, if it's something you enjoy. A garden is much more than a place in which to work. It's a place to live.

## PLANNING A GARDEN ROOM

Let's focus on creating a garden room for a well-balanced, moderately industrious gardener. What do you plan to do in your garden room? In a conventional house, the activities are already assigned by room before we even move in. Their size, shape, fixtures, and location already determine how they're to be used. A stove or a tub is a good indicator. The rooms without appliances give us a little more wiggle room to turn them into something besides a spare bedroom, such as a library, sewing room, or home theater.

A garden room starts from scratch. At the start, the only thing that it has in common with an indoor room is a floor. In most cases, it has no walls, windows, ceilings, furniture, or ornaments. Sometimes, such as in the city, walls of other buildings define the garden space. New

**A former concrete patio slab has been transformed into a peaceful room—perfect for knitting—
with the addition of brick pavers, comfy wicker, and pots of blue lily-of-the-Nile.**

Yorkers know all about this. But many people simply have a "yard," which is usually the lawn, trees, and shrubs that surround the house. The closest most yards get to having a room is the patio, oftentimes a concrete afterthought tacked onto the back of the house.

A real garden room can serve as an extension of the home. Your lifestyle will help you decide how it should be designed, whether for dining, entertaining, catnapping, or all of the above. Creating one room leads to another. Any garden appears larger when it's segmented and all is not apparent at first glance. Other garden rooms can be simply for display, showcasing a collection of plants the way we display trophies, books, and figurines inside. Taking the concept of a room too literally, collectors sometimes find a way to clutter it up with non-plant items. Take the case of an elderly couple I once saw on British TV who collected more than 500 gnomes. The broadcast showed them demolishing their collection with sledgehammers. When asked why, the lady of the house replied, "It got to be a bit much, really." I'm sure there's a lesson for all of us in this.

Getting back to the business of creating a room, the only thing that is absolutely necessary is a sense of enclosure. This can start perhaps with a wall or walls of a building and include fences, pillars, planters, and screens as well as living elements such as hedges and potted plants. Most of us don't like to sit in a room without windows (except at the movies) so the enclosure doesn't need to be thorough. A garden room doesn't necessarily need a ceiling, but it becomes more intimate with some sort of canopy, whether it's a tree, arbor, pergola, or even an umbrella.

> **I'd rather dine in a garden than in the fanciest restaurant in the world.**

## DINING IN THE GARDEN

When I picture creating a garden room, I think about food. I'd rather dine in a garden than in the fanciest restaurant in the world. For one thing, I'm already dressed for it. For another, a summer's evening breeze scented by lilies or angel's trumpets enhances any meal (even one I cook). But even great tastes and scents are secondary if you're uncomfortable, so consider what you and your guests will sit on for a meal in an outdoor dining room. Teak, wrought iron, and cast aluminum—they're all great choices, depending on your taste. I don't go in for plastic—it just doesn't fit in with any of my garden concepts—but because this type of furniture is inexpensive, you can use it initially until you can find and afford what you really like. Furniture makes a design statement in a garden dining room. Sometimes it says, "French café," "English tea time," "Southern elegance," or "Laguna Beach lunch." I'm not exactly sure what mine says except maybe, "This looks comfy," mainly due to cushions and pillows. I'm constantly shuttling them inside when rain clouds appear, but they help to set a mood.

Mood is what a garden room is all about. You create it. It's a room like no other, always changing. And what's even better, a little dirt is perfectly acceptable. Some of my favorite moments have been spent in my outdoor dining room, never mind my compulsive gardening and inability to relax. I recall chili on a cold day, a cool salad on a warm night, the excitement of planting containers each spring, and just hanging out with my pets. I love watching the cats stalk butterflies and the dogs snoozing under the table or "helping" me with watering and deadheading.

A garden room isn't just about entertaining and relaxing. I don't relax much in the vegetable and herb room. I sweat. There's a chair and table in the shade to take a break, but the focus here is production. Though some people integrate vegetables and herbs into the rest of the garden, many gardeners like a separate area dedicated to them. Or they put vegetables and flowers for cutting together (a cutting garden). Some of us just find it too difficult to pick from the garden for fear it would spoil the show. I'm reluctant to pick from my main borders, too.

# ■ Beds and Borders

Let's talk about beds and borders. What's the difference? There really isn't much. A bed is usually a flat patch of ground, often carved out of the lawn. Traditionally, it displays bright

**Where no rules apply, annuals, perennials, and shrubs stuff beds (or are they borders?) carved informally from the lawn. The plantings include roses, lupines, black-eyed Susans, penstemons, and dianthus.**

summer annuals, such as petunias and geraniums, commonly known as "bedding" plants. At one time, when Britannia ruled the waves and Queen Victoria sat on the throne of England, bedding was all the rage. You could show off your wealth based on how grand, intricate, and labor-intensive your garden beds were. We don't see much of this in home gardens any longer, but remnants of it linger in municipal parks every summer. Occasionally a town or city will spell out its name in marigolds, for example. A local hotel tried this a couple of years ago using petunias. It was fairly legible as you drove by in early summer, but as the petunias grew and spread, the hotel name became a blur. The Victorians had enormous gardening staffs to snip and clip. At any rate, we don't bed so much these days.

By contrast, we make borders. A border is largely a European concept, especially English, which replaces beds of annuals with beds of perennials. We'll talk about these kinds of plants in detail later in the book, but suffice it to say that perennials live for many years and come up "perennially" each year, while annuals usually live up to their name and must be planted anew each year. By the very word "border," you might imagine that this piece of ground borders something, such as a wall, walkway, or property line. It can, of course, border something, but it's come to mean an arrangement of perennials usually in long, rectangular expanses. My "borders" are really just two equal strips of earth about 60' by 10' with a path down the middle. Some people like lawns running down their borders or a layer of fine pea gravel that crunches as you walk. A border can run alongside a driveway or fence, go uphill if it has to, and it doesn't even have to be straight. Borders traditionally have some sort of backing to them such as a wall or hedge. A lot of the English ones employ romantically crumbling brick walls. Mine has a picket fence. Whatever it is, the backing serves as a sort of device like a picture frame to set off the beauty of the plants.

> Most of us are essentially cottage gardeners when we start, and after years of experimentation—becoming increasingly sophisticated—we often return to our cottage roots.

Though a border used to be strictly about perennials, it's come to include just about every kind of plant you'd like to toss in it. This "mixed border" concept is a boon to kitchen-sink gardeners like me who wish to incorporate roses, tulips, basil, and anything else we fancy.

The most important part about a border is its complete lack of regimentation. This means no rows and essentially no strict rules. A beautiful border does, however, need a bit of discipline both in its planning and maintenance to keep from looking chaotic. For that we'll discuss colors, shapes, textures, and the sequence of blooms—later.

You've probably heard about "cottage gardens" as much as borders. They're planted just about the same as borders, really, but I'd say that they're especially exuberant and expressive. A famous British garden writer once called cottage gardens "undisciplined masses of flopping vegetation." When they became all the rage, he wrote a glowing book about them. Most of us are essentially cottage gardeners when we start, and after years of experimentation—becoming increasingly sophisticated—we often return to our cottage roots. I used to care far more about clever combinations. Last summer, I accidentally grew a blood red dahlia in a pot with magenta petunias, chartreuse sweet potato vine, and orange cigar plant. It was absolutely hideous and I didn't give a hoot. I'm definitely back to my exuberant cottage phase.

# ■ Rocks in the Garden

Rock gardeners are just cottage gardeners with rocks. They specialize in smaller plants, often from mountainous areas, that grow best amongst rocks, especially in the crevices. Rock gardeners almost always display meticulous grooming techniques as well as a huge thirst to try new plants. Gardening with rocks is a bit different than pure rock gardening. Many people garden with natural rock formations on their properties. Others haul in rocks to pay homage to the natural landscape of their regions.

My sister and I did this—in our own ways—when we were kids. On family trips to the mountains, we were allowed to bring home rocks we collected. Betty and I managed some fairly large-sized rocks that we put in the back of our family station wagon. We saved those for our rock gardens, which we planted with creeping phlox and hen and chicks and populated with

**Stone, wood, and water characterize a Japanese-inspired garden,
with breathtaking water lilies inviting reflection.**

our pet turtles. My sister and I built rock gardens all over the place. It's great to have gardening parents who don't worry about what the neighbors think of their children's latest creation.

Japanese and Chinese styles of gardens often employ rocks in their designs, but for entirely different reasons than creating plant habitats. Many gardeners enjoy bringing Asian elements into their home gardens, as well as evoking the styles of planting. Stone, wood, and water can be used in many ways to evoke an Asian look. One word of caution: the architecture of your home must lend itself to these styles. Simplicity of line and ornament is critical to do justice to your interpretation of a Japanese garden surrounding your home. My understanding is that Japanese gardens, in particular, serve as artistic microcosms of the natural world. Before you do a sand garden or throw up a teahouse, investigate this discipline of gardening thoroughly. As with European styles of gardening, use plants suitable to your region in an Asian-inspired garden.

# ■ Naturalistic Gardens

Wherever you live, you'll find gardens that mirror the natural landscape. One of the strongest garden movements today is about prairies, plains, and meadows. There aren't many left of the virgin grasslands that used to cover so much of this continent. Cornfields and pastures have largely supplanted the plains. I have a particular appreciation for the plants I grew up with on the plains. From the edge of town where we lived, an endless sea of grasses stretched to the horizon.

Prairie and meadow gardens strive to present the beauty of these habitats. Besides the predominant grasses, these gardens also feature many of the wildflowers that, because of their toughness and beauty, have become garden stalwarts throughout the world, such as Indian blanket, goldenrod, aster, gayfeather, and coreopsis.

Most flowers were once wild, except for those "bred in captivity." Through breeding and selection, plants from around the world have blossomed into the ones that we grow in our gardens today. Hybrid tea roses, for example, aren't to be found just growing down by the side of the ditch. As "wild" subjects, many forerunners of modern hybrids look quite different. Modern dahlias, zinnias, and marigolds (all native to Mexico) have become big, bold, and brassy in comparison to the original wild plants. For many gardeners, the charm of the originals far outweighs the "improvements" by breeders.

These are what we usually think of when we picture wildflowers. They vary from region to region, of course, with some having a very large range and others being quite localized. Many

A rustic fence is all that separates these "captive" columbines from the untamed woods beyond; seedlings will likely jump the fence in the coming years.

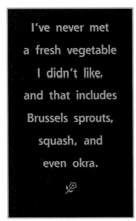

I've never met a fresh vegetable I didn't like, and that includes Brussels sprouts, squash, and even okra.

gardeners enjoy going "native," planting and growing the wild species of their regions. Already adapted to your soil and climate, they will probably prove to be tough and enduring.

# ■ Garden Edibles

Despite the fact that this introduction to gardening does not focus on edible plants, I wanted to be sure to offer a few tips to those of you who will not be content with a strictly ornamental garden. Growing up in a gardening family gave me an appreciation for working in the soil, even at a very early age, and for more than just growing plants. I also liked hoeing rows, planting seeds, and especially harvesting. Kids are notoriously fussy about eating vegetables (and often turn into fussy adults). But children in gardening families never need to be prodded to eat their peas, beets, or beans.

I've never met a fresh vegetable I didn't like, and that includes Brussels sprouts, squash, and even okra. I salivate just writing about homegrown corn and tomatoes. The popularity of farmer's markets testifies to our appreciation of freshly picked vegetables. As soon as a vegetable is picked, its sugar begins to turn to starch and the flavor fades. Carrots, corn, and peas are decidedly more delicious if eaten straight from the garden (or, in my case, in the garden; peas rarely make it to the kitchen).

Taste isn't the only reason to raise your own vegetables. With the tremendous popularity of pesticide-free, organically grown produce, it makes sense to raise your own healthy crops. The key is not to panic at the arrival of the first aphid. You can manage outbreaks of pests using soap. That's right, soap. Pure garden soap that you mix with water is available at garden centers. It doesn't poison insects, but instead dissolves their hard exoskeletons. Like the Wicked Witch of the West, they melt away. Explain that to your kids and they'll be thrilled to help spray the soap.

While pests are always a cause of concern, the most important aspect of growing vegetables is your soil. Although a loose, friable (crumbly) soil is ideal, a lack of it doesn't mean you're out of luck. Homeowners with heavy clay soil and high-rise dwellers without any soil at all have options. Raised beds filled with fertile topsoil can be created, and heavy soils can be improved by incorporating organic matter. And almost anybody with a balcony that receives at least a half-day's sun can grow vegetables in containers.

Root crops such as beets, turnips, carrots, onions, and radishes grow best in very loose soil with the consistency of store-bought potting soil. They have a difficult time extending their roots into heavy or rocky soil. Raised beds and large containers provide that ideal, loose growing medium.

As you plan your vegetable garden, choose a spot that receives plenty of sun. Some people don't consider a vegetable garden very pretty and hide it behind the garage or along the alley. Don't fall into that trap. Find the best spot for growing vegetables and turn it into a beautiful space. It can hold its own as a viable garden room if you enclose it with nice fencing or hedges, dress it up with ornaments such as a birdbath (birds should always be welcome to dine on insects), and create an interesting layout with paths and paving. Trellises and arbors add further architectural interest and support climbers such as pole beans, peas, and squash. Many gardeners add flowers to their vegetable garden, especially edible ones such as pansies, nasturtiums, and sweet Williams.

Vegetables are split into two groups: cool-season and warm-season. At the beginning of the growing season (cool season), depending on where you live, you can plant seeds or transplant young nursery seedlings of lettuce, spinach, peas, beets, radishes, and onions. They can withstand a light frost—even snow—and develop rapidly during cool, sunny weather. When the real heat hits (warm season), spinach and lettuce will bolt (send up flowering stalks), and their useful-ness is over. Radishes become bitter and woody and peas cease flowering and become magnets for spider mites. Pull up these cool-season plants and compost them, and plant heat-loving vegeta-bles in their place. Warm soil is essential for beans, corn, and squash to germinate well.

More tomatoes succumb to bad judgment about timing than any other crop. Peppers are right up there, too. Don't jump the gun: One unseasonably hot day doesn't mean it's safe to plant your warm-season crops. Tomatoes and peppers grow so quickly that even those planted in early June in northern gardens and in mountainous areas will rapidly catch up and soon surpass plants set out too early. Neither can stand one degree below freezing, and cool nights will stunt their growth for the entire season. Pay attention to the night temperatures in your area—they must stay reliably above 50 degrees; daily highs are irrelevant.

My best tip for growing great tomatoes (the favorite of most gardeners) is to bury a young transplant all the way up to its set of lower leaves. Tomatoes root all along the stem this way, ensuring a sturdy, well-rooted plant. Keep the soil evenly moist, feed regularly with a fertilizer formulated especially for tomatoes, and pick and stomp pesky tomato hornworms. Nothing beats the taste of a homegrown tomato. Each bite is memorable. I can almost taste it now.

# ■ Container Gardening

For everything you want to grow but don't think you can, there's container gardening. You control the soil, fertilizer, and water to accommodate most any plant you've been hankering to grow. The 300 pots on my patio and balcony are a testament to a lot of hankering.

Start with large pots of at least 10" or 12" diameters. Any smaller and you'll never be able to keep the soil within them moist (my small pots get good use housing my collection of succulents and cactus, which don't need much water). Terra-cotta pots "breathe," meaning that their porous walls allow both air and moisture to penetrate the walls. While that's beneficial to roots, it's not so good if the pots dry out on a hot day when you're not home. Containers made of fiberglass, wood, plastic, and glazed pottery don't breathe and consequently hold moisture better. Use potting soil (bags of commercially available soil labeled "potting soil" can be found at any nursery or garden supply store); garden soil rarely makes a suitable growing medium in pots.

> With container gardening you control the soil, fertilizer, and water to accommodate most any plant you've been hankering to grow.

You can create beautiful combinations of plants by blending upright, rounded, and trailing plants for a balanced effect. Plant them very tightly together for a lush look right off the bat. Fertilize every week to ten days to get great "magazine cover" results. Some plants may be best grown as single specimens in their own pots. They can then be grouped with other pots. I use bricks, blocks, and overturned pots beneath my

A low stone wall elevates pots of flowers for an up-close experience, including oxalis, pink spider lily, pale pink Asiatic lilies, magenta stock, and white alstroemeria.

containers to stage them for the best show. I try to get many of them up to eye level so I can enjoy them when I'm dining or writing. Conversely, lower your hanging baskets so you're not just staring at the bottom of the basket.

Individual pots or groupings of them serve as focal points in the garden, disguise eyesores, direct traffic flow, provide screening, and mainly beautify our outdoor living spaces. Though we think of container plantings essentially for summer color, they're useful anytime, not only in frost-free climates but in cold ones as well. Holly, evergreens, and ornamental grasses can be especially attractive with a light dusting of snow. Also, containers can host dwarf fruit trees, evergreens, flowering shrubs, bulbs, and almost everything else that is ordinarily grown in the ground. (Rooftop and balcony gardeners need big pots and planters for some of these options.)

## ■ Watery Effects

A pond, reflecting pool, or fountain serves as cooling relief from summer's heat and glare. Gardeners' ponds play a vital role for birds, both for drinking and bathing. Even if you have no intention of ever installing a water feature in your garden, at least provide a bowl of clean water. The birds will revel in it and repay you by eating your unwanted insects.

When you do take the plunge and become a water gardener, you'll enter an exciting new world with its own lingo. Soon, you'll talk liners, pumps, filters, fish, and algae like a pro. You'll fall in love with water lilies and my favorite, the lotus. With its graceful blue-green leaves and elegant pink flowers, it's no wonder the lotus was used by ancient Egyptians as a recurring artistic motif.

Beyond water lilies and lotus, a pond may host many beautiful aquatics, especially those plants that thrive at water's edge. Some are hardy and may be planted directly in the mucky soil where their roots stay perpetually wet, while others are kept in their pots and submerged below water level. Among the loveliest of these plants are Japanese and Louisiana irises as well as *Iris pseudacorus*, the fabled yellow fleur-de-lis of France. Rushes, reeds, and cattails are also perfect for the water's edge, along with tropical elephant ears (*Colocasia*), pickerel, papyrus, and water cannas. The dramatic foliage of rodgersias and ligularias can be stunning, topped by pink or golden flowers, respectively. Some water plants simply float. Water hyacinth, water lettuce, and duckweed migrate around the pond with the breeze. The first two should only be allowed in enclosed ponds, as they have become major pests in the South, escaping into and clogging waterways.

Deciding what sort of water feature you want is the most important part. It takes a deft touch to pull off a naturalistic pond. Unless you have a lot of space (in full sun, by the way), it's difficult to make your pond convincing. How many of us city dwellers have a natural spring and a rock outcropping in our backyards? In the country or where there are hills and rock formations, the illusion is far more convincing, but a more formal approach may work best for most of us.

**A convincingly naturalistic pond teems with life such as an orange canna, rushes, water lilies, and golden yellow ligularia.**

My raised pond, about 4' by 8', doesn't pretend to be natural. It has provided me with hours of entertainment as well as some strange encounters. You may meet some big birds. Herons may come for a tasty meal. A light on your pond at night is the equivalent of the famed golden arches to night-flying herons. Some water gardeners resort to netting over their ponds, but the best idea comes from my friends Susan and Rhonda, who bought black plastic boxes (about the size of a bread box) at a home improvement store. The boxes, intended for some sort of plumbing, have holes for tubes and pipes so the fish can swim in and out and hide inside. It works like a charm.

Raccoons regularly mug my pond. Whether it's to wash or eat (there always seem to be fewer fish after one of their visits), they just trash my pond. I put mousetraps on the pond's edge to deter them. The fish population seems to rebound from the predations and only once have I needed to start from scratch. Several winters ago, a warm day lured my goldfish to the surface. The temperature plunged suddenly, trapping them in the ice. This is known as the "great fish stick episode." The adventure continues.

# ■ Color Basics

We've talked plenty about plants, although barely mentioning what draws us to them: color. We're all so different. And we see color differently. Some of us are cautious or confused about color. Others, like me, tend to collect one or two kinds of plants and give scant thought to color combinations. Then there are the magpies, who are attracted to bright, shiny objects, and have one of everything. There are also the minimalists, whose color palette is extremely limited. And finally, there are those with a "survival garden," where the color scheme is based on what hasn't died.

Unfortunately, too many of us never find out what we really like because we're scared to experiment. Whether it's our home, wardrobe, or garden, we're so unsure and afraid of making mistakes that we limit ourselves before we even start. Many people stick with the equivalent of a black cocktail dress. They play it safe.

Comparing colors of apparel and garden flowers isn't quite fair, but I think people confuse them. You have no idea how many times I've heard a client say, "I hate orange," or "I loathe yellow." It's too bad that somewhere between our first box of crayons and adulthood we learned to hate a particular color. I have to respect this prejudice, of course, but on what is it based? If it's because you look hideous in yellow or orange, don't wear it. Clothing is next to our skin and hair; flowers bloom against a green background.

> **To begin experimenting with color, take one base color and repeat it over and over in your plantings.**

Coats of color paint the garden throughout the season. Planning helps to match them with the appropriate time. Our psychological needs should be considered in the process. In northern states, for example, gardeners are hungry—no, ravenous—for spring color after a monochromatic winter. In summer, blues and lavenders provide a slight respite from the heat. And in fall, gold and orange match our moods, even if they might seem out of sync at any other time. There's no reason to exclude any color from the garden; just find the season where it best fits.

The palette of spring plantings can be among the weirdest. Maybe it's because the fall-planted bulbs aren't ever compared with the perennials with which they'll bloom until they erupt into a big spring clash. After all, a tulip is just a picture on a bag when we plant it. Small wonder that some combinations are excessively cheerful. Red tulips and basket-of-gold are the visual equivalents of nails on a chalkboard to me. Yellow daffodils and hot pink creeping phlox I find equally disturbing. I actually like this perennial and employ it frequently, especially soft pink 'Candy Stripe' and 'Emerald Blue', although the latter is so deceivingly named. Its color is delicate lavender-blue. (The color peacemakers in the garden are blue, purple, or lavender.) I've usually found that almost all pastels go together without much trouble and that all intense colors—let's call them jewel tones—work well together.

Because color can be so personal and so emotional, I don't believe in assigning rules about it. Even if I did, I also believe that rules are for breaking. There are some tips, however,

Pretty in pink, these Asiatic lilies, pincushion flowers, and rose campion get a boost from the chartreuse leaves of variegated yucca and golden hops vine.

that can help a bit when approaching color. To begin experimenting with color, take one base color and repeat it over and over in your plantings. This is similar to painting the walls of a room with a consistent color. Since we were discussing lavender-blue anyway, consider how soothing it is and how many perennials and shrubs feature lavender-blue flowers, from veronicas and catmints to salvias and butterfly bushes. This color can span the seasons, providing a base for adding bolder jewel tones.

The same base color could be pink, yellow, or white. Then you can go off in any direction that suits you and the season. In the case of lavender-blue, add some deeper blues and purples and you've set the stage for hot pink or coral accents, or perhaps even orange. Oddly enough, if you take the base colors of pink, yellow, or white and add darker blues and purples, you've set up exactly the same situation. A base color plus purple is the ideal way to incorporate jewel tones into the garden, whether they're golden California poppies, ruby roses, magenta wine cups (*Callirhoe involucrata*), or orange tiger lilies.

The base color idea is also practical for those who collect plants that span a wide color range, such as irises or lilies. Sometimes these flowers come in unusual shades—or several at one time—that are a bit hard to fit in gracefully. A simple base color background pulls it all together. For the magpie gardeners, who are attracted to bright colors and pick up one of this and one of that until their gardens look like button collections, add a base color to make some semblance of order out of the hodgepodge. This could be as simple as broadcasting (i.e., spreading) a half pound of bachelor's buttons or sweet alyssum seeds (in a single color, not a mix) to fill in the gaps and provide unity.

Minimalist schemes are often great experiments—in the beginning. If you create a garden room that's limited in color (and you become as tired of it as I became of my all-white border), try adding the equivalent of throw pillows. Toss in one new color each season—even if it's just a foliage contrast—such as lime green in an all-yellow garden or burgundy in all-pink or -red one.

Finally—and you know who you are—there are those with a color scheme based on what's left from what you planted last year. Plenty of gardens start out with lovely color schemes, but the voles ate the tulips, the daisies croaked last winter, and the astilbe succumbed during the drought. What's left doesn't hang together. I've seen living rooms like this too. The walls used to match the sofa that the cat shredded, and the new chintz chairs were such a great deal, even though they're not that great with the plaid upholstery on the new sofa.

Let's make it simple. Pick one accent foliage color, such as silver, and three colors (make one of them bright) say pale pink, powder blue, and magenta. If you've already planted, dig out everything that doesn't fit this scheme and give these strays to your neighbors. Go to the nursery. Splurge.

# ■ Think Ahead When Buying

Keep in mind that summer and fall flowers are not in bloom in spring; two-thirds of your purchases should be for coming seasons. Spring may seem like an odd time to plan for fall color in the garden, but each autumn we do the reverse, planting crocuses, daffodils, and tulips to greet us in spring. It makes sense to take advantage of our early-season enthusiasm to ensure a colorful garden late in the year.

Summer heat often puts a damper on planting. If it's hot and/or dry, it's both tiring and risky to plant perennials. And let's face it: We buy what's in bloom. Most people purchase their plants in spring. Blooming annuals and perennials fly off the garden center shelves. The gallon pots of later-blooming perennials, devoid of bloom, get passed by. If you truly want a profusion of bloom throughout the season, a full half of your spring purchases should be strictly green. That's right, no flowers. To do this, you need to do some homework. What late bloomers are suitable for your garden?

People who need instant gratification will need to steel themselves. It's difficult to resist color. If you buy smart, your garden will be as beautiful in September as in June, if not more so. Don't forget the crescendo effect: by combining annuals with late-blooming perennials, the color will intensify throughout the summer and into fall. Many annuals reach their peaks in late August and September, coinciding with the explosion of fall-blooming perennials. Annual zinnias, dahlias, gomphrenas, verbenas, sweet potato vines, and black-eyed Susans hit their stride just as perennial asters, mums, hummingbird trumpets, plumbagos, coneflowers, Japanese anemones, and ornamental grasses come into their own.

Planting late bloomers in spring gives them almost an entire season to grow and perform. Even small-sized plants, with proper care, can put on a great show, although they'll be even more amazing in coming years. There's an old saying about perennials: "The first year they sleep, the second year they creep, the third year they leap." They may leap a little faster than the old adage—depending on the attention and fertilizer you lavish upon them—but have patience for a year or two.

# ■ Weed Strategies

Dreams do come true in fairy tales (and sometimes in gardens), but it's usually after plenty of toil and suffering. In fairy tales, the usual cause of all the turmoil is the wicked stepmother. In gardens, it's the weeds. During the excitement of planning and planting, weeds aren't on our minds. We're dreaming of tulips and roses and tomatoes. How dare weeds give us a wake-up call?!

Everyone wants a magic "cure" for weeds. For the kind of garden I like and design, there isn't one. I don't use or recommend black plastic, landscape fabric, weed barrier cloth, or smothering bark nuggets. They're just not natural. The only way to achieve a real garden is with real sweat. And that means weeding.

Weeds are a fact of life. Whenever we turn a spadeful of earth, we're exposing opportunistic seeds. Developing a strategy for coping with them is part of making a new garden or enlarging an existing one. In one category are the really bad, horrible weeds. Whoever said that a weed is just a flower growing in the wrong spot must have been on heavy medication or never ran into the likes of bindweed, kudzu, bittersweet, thistle, and various ivies. You probably know about the worst thugs in your neighborhood. They're basically despised for their aggression, tenacity, and deep roots. In the other category are the pesky weeds, slightly less aggravating because of their annual nature. These include portulaca, wild lettuce, shepherd's purse, mare's tail, lamb's quarters, hen bit, dandelion, pigweed, and knotweed. It's funny that so many carry picturesque—even cute—common names. Their greatest strength is in their numbers—kajillions of them.

I've never had the good fortune to start one of my own gardens on a piece of property that didn't host a couple of really bad thugs. Sometimes they've even fooled me into thinking I'd conquered them, only to discover they were just waiting until I'd planted before rearing their ugly heads again. My best piece of advice is to make sure they're good and dead before you plant. The method of killing them is up to you and depends on the nature of the villains.

The worst possible thing to do is to rototill if you're facing a persistent, deep-rooted weed such as bindweed. For a week or so, you'll pat yourself on the back. But soon every piece you chopped up will become a new weed. The best control for these sorts of weeds might be to use an herbicide or to smother them with a layer of plastic or newspapers for up to a year. My personal method is to pull them over and over—up to six times—to weaken the plant, then to hit them with an herbicide such as Round-up. My rampaging crop of bindweed appears to be (nearly) extinct, but the tree of heaven that came with

> Whoever said that a weed is just a flower growing in the wrong spot must have been on heavy medication or never ran into the likes of bindweed, kudzu, bittersweet, thistle, and various ivies.

the place sends out runners as effortlessly as most of us send e-mails. There's even one growing in my laundry room. Yes, in it. I've chopped, dug, and sprayed, but it's a battle of wills. Ordinarily I wouldn't credit a tree with the ability to form intent, but I do wonder when it mounts a home invasion.

When you've conquered the really tough weeds (or if you lucked out and never had to face them at all), the first-year garden still offers challenges. Weeding can take the fun out of the whole experience. It seems never-ending, as weeds of different kinds take their turns and germinate throughout the growing season. Many weed seeds can lie dormant for years or decades, just waiting for an opportunity.

My most persistent of the pesky weeds last season in a new garden area was portulaca. Springing up as thick as dog hair, this fleshy-leafed annual thrives in hot, dry weather, much like its ornamental cousin we usually call moss rose. There was nothing rosy about this picture. Whereas most annuals that I hoe or pluck have the decency to die, portulaca often re-roots. I like to use a tool called an "action" or "shuffle" hoe for annual weeds. It looks a bit like a horseshoe mounted on a handle, with a flat, two-sided blade that cuts just beneath the crust of the soil as you rake it back and forth. It's very useful, but I go back with a rake to pick up the portulaca before it roots again.

I went through about five rounds with the portulaca, cleaning out every last one before a new batch would sprout a week or so later. Cooler temperatures finally turned the tide in my favor, so I expect very little resistance this coming season. The perennials will begin to expand, shading much of the ground, leaving less and less opportunity for portulaca or any other weeds. The third year in a garden for me is generally almost weed-free, leaving more time for the more rewarding chores.

Weeding does have its good points, depending on how efficient you become. There are days I actually enjoy it. Good tools help. A really sturdy dandelion digger is perfect for tap-rooted weeds. Don't buy a cheap one; it won't last a week without bending. I rely heavily on my Japanese fisherman's knife, often called a hori-hori. It can serve for tap-rooted weeds as well as shallow-rooted weeds, because the edge is serrated to cut just below the soil surface. Several kinds of hoes are useful as well, from the previously mentioned hollow type to the standard flat blade or smaller dagger-pointed variety for tight spaces. And some people prefer their bare hands, wrestling victory from the earth in hand-to-hand combat.

Weeding takes up valuable time, so we need to make the most of it. I often play music on headphones. Sometimes I sing. My neighbors frown on this. During the attack of the portulaca, I used the reward system on myself. It goes something like this: "If I get as far as that butterfly bush (or whatever landmark selected), I'll stop for a while, sit in the shade, and possibly find the strength to go inside and find some chocolate." The weeds are gone and I'm still using this system. Now that's a happy ending.

# ■ Insects, Pests, and Diseases in the Garden

My parents never used insecticides in their garden, so I've grown up pretty ignorant of them. And I intend to keep it that way. People freak out at the sight of the first aphid of the year and overreact with an arsenal of chemical weapons. My advice? Chill. A bug-free garden is as unnatural as one made of artificial flowers. As I've mentioned before, soap is a gardener's best friend. I mix a teaspoon of Dr. Bronner's Castille Oil soap in a spray bottle with a quart of water and have at it. Spraying any pesky aphids I can see (you've got to hit them for the soap to dissolve them), I also make sure to hit the undersides of leaves and stems. This is where most sucking insects like aphids, spider mites, and white flies hang out.

Then there are the chewing insects like caterpillars, beetles, and earwigs. I hate earwigs. It's not that they do any more damage than any other bug; it's just that they're furtive like cockroaches with little pincers in front. I've seen enough science fiction movies to be totally creeped out by the threat they could pose to all humanity.

For every bad bug in the garden, there's one on your side. And along with the ladybugs, lacewings, predatory wasps, praying mantis, and spiders (the good guys) is the bird and bat brigade, which feasts on insects. Start to tinker with this coalition by introducing poisons, and you'll destroy the natural balance. Would you begrudge the caterpillars a meal or two before they transform into butterflies? And no matter how careful you are with chemical sprays and dusts, do you really want to take chances with children, pets, fish, and wildlife?

Of course, there may be critters that you would like to banish from your garden. Depending on where you live, perhaps you'll tangle with mice, squirrels, voles, moles, ground squirrels, gophers, rabbits, skunks, raccoons, deer, elk, or moose—or some combination thereof. Consult your local experts at botanical gardens, nurseries, and extension services on how best to deal with whatever is plaguing you. There are some truly destructive insects and critters out there with which I've never had to deal. Perhaps you may need to at some point. All I can say is that I'd urge you to take the most conservative approach. It never hurts to consult the seasoned gardeners in your neighborhood. Odds are, they've seen it all and may have some clever, environmentally friendly remedies. Approaches work differently in some regions and at certain times of the year.

Some of your staunchest allies are your pets. Both cats and dogs can be deterrents to wildlife, whether they're aggressive protectors or just hanging out on the porch. The mere scent of dogs, for example, puts off deer. I met a man in Montana with a beautiful garden out in the country that wasn't fenced (usually the only reliable way to keep deer out). He'd trained his dog since he was a puppy to mark certain trees and rocks that ringed the property. He and the puppy walked and peed several times a day for several months until it became part of the dog's daily routine.

Still, I'd recommend fencing for best results, since deer will eat the shingles off your house if they're hungry enough. Much is made of deer-resistant plants that they will find unpalatable, as well as soap sprays, hot pepper sprays, blood meal, sirens, flashing lights, and heavy metal music. I'd imagine you'd mostly alarm your neighbors rather than have a lasting effect on a herd of deer with appetites bigger than those of teenagers. I think deer are beautiful creatures when I see them in the mountains, but I can't imagine them grazing in my garden. I think they'd quickly lose their charm. So put up some substantial fencing or get a puppy and go for a stroll.

Plant diseases are no fun. Some are not usually life-threatening, such as mildew, although others such as clematis wilt are fatal. Can you prevent most diseases? Not really. Can you avoid the plants that get them? You bet. Nursing sick plants is grim and depressing. A garden full of mildewed, black-spotted plants is common, but unnecessary. In any region there are hundreds, no thousands, of plants that stay healthy no matter how humid and muggy it gets. Some books will recommend "good air circulation," as if you could place giant fans in pertinent spots in your garden. When plants succumb to disease, they're most likely ill-suited to growing in your region. You can become nursemaid rather than gardener or decide that no matter how lovely a plant might be (somewhere else) you can find a new love. And it's always worth investigating varieties that have natural resistance or have been bred to be resistant.

# ■ Realistic Maintenance

How much work your garden requires depends on its size, complexity, and the types of plants you grow. It also depends on your temperament. Some of us can easily overlook flaws. Others have this compulsive need to be on top of everything all the time, so we're constantly snipping and clipping. And timing is everything.

When I was five years old, my family moved to a small town on the eastern plains of Colorado. Gardening was a hard-fought battle on that windswept land. My early memories are of flowers, from the lilac and bridal veil bushes that hugged our house, to tulips and tomatoes in the garden, to wild roses and asters in the fields next to our house.

I've gardened for more decades than I care to admit, and it's still a sweaty and dirty business; but I no longer think in terms of war. Fighting nature is an exercise in futility. Accepting soil and weather conditions—and welcoming challenges—yields the most rewards. Knowing what to do—and when—makes gardening a pleasure rather than a chore (depending, of course, on how you feel about sweat and dirt).

Each spring I observe great mistakes. Apartment dwellers imagine their houseplants would appreciate a little sunshine as much as they do and drag them to the balcony; ficus trees and ferns bake to a crisp. Blooming delphiniums and roses fresh from the greenhouse get planted in suburban gardens way too early; a late snowstorm inevitably flattens them like pancakes.

The trickiest time of the gardening season begins in midspring. The key is to balance enthusiasm with caution. Starved for color after our winter abstinence, some of us plant recklessly without consulting the calendar. Each region has a set date considered to be that of the average last frost. In my region, May 15 is the green light to set out warm-season favorites such as tomatoes, peppers, marigolds, and zinnias. But May 15 doesn't come with a guarantee, and it's actually too late for the cool-season annuals such as peas, spinach, leaf lettuce, and pansies. This will likely prove true in your region as well.

In truth, the gardening season begins much earlier than most people think and ends much later as well. Learning what gets planted when—and where—is vitally important. Novice gardeners try to buy tulip bulbs in spring, never guessing that their window of opportunity closed in late fall. Sun-loving roses languish beneath a canopy of trees, while shade-loving hostas fry in a sunny hot spot. Yankees who move down south stick to their old habits and plant their pansies just in time to roast them to a crisp. There's no need. We all make mistakes, and good gardeners learn from them. Just avoid the obvious ones. If you're not killing some plants from time to time, you're not trying very hard to learn how to garden. Experience, of course, is the best teacher. I still kill my fair share of plants; it's just more embarrassing for me.

Perhaps we should talk a bit about shopping before we talk about the art of planting and the other garden skills. Shopping is one of my favorite parts of gardening. You say you're good at it? You'll make a great gardener. Shop in stores throughout the season and from winter catalogs

Imagine the pleasure of tending this productive plot devoted to squash and corn, as well as to flowers for cutting—cosmos, marigolds, and sunflowers.

and your garden will never be dull. I rarely see crummy, poorly grown plants at a nursery these days, so I'm not going to go into a long spiel about selecting healthy plants. Look for good foliage color and you might check beneath the leaves for bugs—but I don't do that, so why should you? There will probably be a few roots poking out from the drainage holes in the bottom of the plant's pot. That's fine. If they're longer than a few inches and the root ball is threatening to bust out, the plant is known as "pot bound." This hasn't ever stopped me from buying a plant. You simply take it home, cut it out of its plastic prison, and try to trim and help separate the roots a bit. Then give it a loving home in the ground or a new pot.

## ■ Basic Skills

There are a few basic skills to learn to become a good gardener. They're all easily mastered. Most become second nature in time. Intuition plays a big part in figuring out what to do and

> Whoever writes nursey tags for plants lives in a Camelot of gardening where plants reach amazing proportions never seen elsewhere.

when. Avoid making work for yourself. If everything looks all right, let sleeping dogs lie. Don't go out and hack at your bushes just because you think you should be doing something.

## PLANTING

Planting is the most important skill you can learn. Do it gently, but firmly. The best way to learn is to watch an experienced gardener at work. Go to a botanical garden if there's one nearby to observe. Better yet, volunteer so you can get hands-on experience.

To plant your newly purchased plants, dig a hole larger than the pots in which they came. Turn the pots upside down with one hand, holding the other hand underneath to catch them, and coax the plants out gently (gravity will do most of the work); no yanking and pulling out by the stems. Plant them at the same level that they're growing in their pots, but in a slight depression. Gently pack the soil around the plant, but no stomping. Just use the strength in your hands.

As you work, build a little mud wall about 2" high around each plant to capture moisture. "Puddle in" each plant with a very slow trickle of the hose until it's thoroughly saturated. Each plant is essentially still in its container, so water deeply each time, probably every four to seven days for a gallon-size perennial, depending on your soil and weather. If you live in a cold winter area, fertilize every couple of weeks through July, and then stop so the plants can begin to prepare for cooler fall weather. In their second year, perennials need little or no fertilizer.

## TRANSPLANTING

There comes a time when you'll want to divide and transplant a perennial. This is best done in early spring just as the plant emerges, but hardly anybody gets around to it then. You can basically do it any time except during the real summer heat. Dig it up (a digging fork is easiest, but a shovel will do). Cut it in half or in several pieces depending on its size. The blade of a spade works well. Give it a hard thrust. You can also use a sturdy kitchen knife.

Transplanting is just like planting, except that you usually give your subject a haircut before you replant. This generally means cutting back the top growth so the roots don't have so much to support while they're reestablishing themselves. The plant should end up at the same level it was growing at before you started. Again, create an earthen dam around the base to catch and hold water and thoroughly soak the soil immediately after planting.

## GROWING FROM SEED

Sowing seeds is much less work than planting. Some kinds can be simply sprinkled over the soil as if you were feeding chickens. I usually do this in either fall or late winter with annuals such as larkspurs, poppies, and bachelor's buttons. Vegetable seeds are usually but not always planted in rows, at the appropriate time for each kind. After digging and leveling the site with a rake, use a hoe to create a furrow 1" or so deep. Then plant the corn, peas, beans, or whatever you like, covering the seeds about a ¼" to ½" deep. Space the seeds a few inches apart, knowing that as they germinate and grow, you'll need to thin them to allow room for each one to develop. How much to thin depends on what you're growing. Radishes need only a few inches in between, while corn needs a foot.

Sowing seeds inside is a bit easier, mainly because you're sitting down. The easiest way for most of us is to fill plastic six-pack plant containers with a soil mixture especially formulated for seedlings. Plant a few seeds per cell (you'll need to thin later), covering them as directed on the seed packet. Water from the bottom by soaking the containers in their trays or you'll probably wash the seeds all over the place. Seed packets also tell you when to plant, generally four to eight weeks before the average frost-free date in your area, so count backward from that date. It helps to get this all organized on paper in midwinter, plus it gives us something to dream about when winter seems never-ending.

## SPACING PLANTS

How much room your plants need between them is very tricky. I pay attention to the growth estimates for trees and shrubs and space accordingly. For perennials and annuals, I tend to follow my own instincts because I don't trust the nursery tags. Whoever writes them lives in a far-off Camelot land of gardening where plants reach amazing proportions never seen elsewhere. So for where I live in the mountain West, I cut the recommended spacing down by at least a third and sometimes by half. My theory is that most of us prefer results during our lifetimes.

**Glorious dahlias result from pinching, staking, fertilizing, and deadheading. They're worth the fuss.**

## FEEDING PLANTS

Once everything is planted and growing, feed your plants. There's no set standard; some plants are heavier feeders than others. Some don't want or need any supplemental fertilization at all. Just as a general guideline, be generous with roses, bulbs, most annuals, containerized plants, and vegetables. Most trees, shrubs, vines, herbs, and perennials can get along pretty well on their own. Many people overfeed their perennials and end up with a bunch of lax, floppy plants. Then they have to stake them. I don't like staking and I rarely grow plants that are bred to fall over, but occasionally I make an exception. You probably will, too.

## PLANT SUPPORTS

My weakness is dahlias. The tall ones need stakes. I grow them in pots on my patio for their huge, eye-popping blossoms in the heat of summer and into fall. I pinch my dahlias when they're about 6" tall. This means I tweak out the growing tip with my thumb and forefinger. This causes them to branch out and get bushy. Pinching is great to help avoid tall thin plants. Try it on petunias, flowering tobacco, pansies, flowering maples, and geraniums to get really floriferous plants. But back to stakes. When necessary—and before your lanky plant blows over—insert at the base a sturdy bamboo pole as tall as the plant is projected to reach. Use yarn, string, or twist-ties every 10", attaching it first to the stake and then around the plant stem. Sometimes I use tree branches with a "Y" joint (like one you'd use to make a sling-shot) and simply prop up a droopy plant. This kind of staking is barely noticeable. You can also buy metal supports and hoops. These are useful for top-heavy flowers such as peonies, which too often display their blossoms in the mud.

## DEADHEADING, SHAPING, AND PRUNING

Most plants need grooming. The most common cleanup is deadheading, which has nothing to do with concerts. It's simply cutting or pinching off faded blossoms and their stems. The technique varies. For a Shasta daisy, for example, take off the flower and its long stem where it emerges from the base of leaves. For a begonia, just pinch off the spent flower. Deadheading encourages plants to keep blooming rather than putting their energies into seed production. Sometimes the entire plant is cut back to persuade it to regenerate and re-bloom. These summer cutbacks are for June bloomers that look tired and worn out in July. Now's your chance to do some serious whacking, cutting back many perennials by half or more—sometimes all the way to the ground. A list of candidates that prosper after a cutback (and a subsequent feeding) include many daisies, meadow sage, lupine, columbine, and catmint.

You can always do a bit of shaping and pruning when you like, but most people do too much. For most of us, early spring is the best time to cut out dead branches on trees and shrubs and do minimal shaping. This is also the time to cut back perennials and ornamental grasses. Meadows can simply be mowed. The old idea that the garden needs to be put to bed in fall has pretty much gone by the wayside. Save your autumnal energy for planting bulbs and moving pots of tropical plants inside. Nowadays we leave perennials, grasses, and even some annuals alone as winter comes, the better to enjoy their freeze-dried beauty. This also helps to protect the crowns of the plants from the extremes of winter.

# ■ Tips to Save Energy: Yours and the Garden's

The rhythm of a garden isn't a constant one. Nor is a gardener's. In spring most of us have energy to burn. That's good because there's plenty to be accomplished. Last year's perennials and grasses are cut back in mid- to late winter, depending on where you live. At about the same time, cool-season annuals and vegetables need to be sown outdoors. Peas, for example, are traditionally planted on St. Patrick's Day across the northern tier of states. In the meantime, many gardeners get a jump on the growing season by starting warm-season annuals and vegetables indoors.

The weather plays us like a yo-yo. It's too cold. Then it's warming up. No, wait—it's still too cold. Well, it feels pretty mild; maybe I should start transplanting and spading the vegetable patch. Oops, it's snowing. The moisture was good anyway. Now maybe it's okay. It was still pretty chilly last night. It's been 90 degrees for a week now. Oh dear, is it too late to plant tomatoes? This weather roller coaster can really wear you down. In the beginning of the season (spring, that is) we all invariably overdo it. We're not yet garden tough, so sore muscles and strained backs become common. Our bodies tone and strengthen as the season progresses. By mid-June, we're feeling pretty buff.

> In the beginning of the season (spring, that is) we all invariably overdo it. We're not yet garden tough.

Then it hits. The heat, humidity, grasshoppers, and crabgrass start to take their toll. We've reached the summer energy crisis. In what's supposed to be the time when we most enjoy our gardens, we can become too worn out. It seems only the super-gardener can shrug off the summer's setbacks to keep his or her garden picture-perfect. I'm no super-gardener, but my midsummer garden looks pretty cool. Here's how:

- Water plants in early morning, deeply and only when necessary (remember, poke your fingers into the soil to see how much moisture your plants have).
- Count on container plantings for color and substance (these are the plants you can most easily control); use tropicals and other heat lovers.
- Give your plants plenty of food and water (especially for the container plantings); install drip lines in the garden if you're mechanically inclined.
- Cut back early-blooming perennials.
- Select a different, small area to be groomed each day. Give it 20 minutes or whatever time you can. Move on to a new area the next day.
- Wear light-colored clothing along with broad-brimmed hats when you garden.
- Don't sweat the small stuff, such as deadheading. There's always next week.
- The best time to pull a weed is when you see it.

# ■ Essential Garden Tools

What tools do you need? Forgive me if I say, "It depends." There are some perfectly nice tools I've never used, so I can only tell you what I find "essential" and "nice to have." Let's start with the ones I use most. The Japanese fisherman's knife, called a hori-hori, features a 7" steel blade, serrated on one side, with a wood or plastic handle. Its primary uses include weeding, planting small stuff, and, presumably, gutting fish. A hori-hori costs about $20 to $35 depending on the model you get. Only one major caveat: Keep this tool out of reach of your children!

## PRUNERS AND LOPPERS

The next essential is a pair of pruners, also called secauters by people who don't think pruners is descriptive enough. There are several different styles. I'd suggest a basic pair with a grip that feels comfortable. You'll get plenty of use out of a pair of pruners when you cut back the garden in spring, prune shrubs and small tree branches, deadhead flowers, and harvest herbs. I'd splurge and get a good pair (meaning, lifetime), for which you'll spend close to $50. Loppers are like bigger pruners and can handle slightly larger limbs up to about 1 ½" in diameter. They're nice to have around (I borrow my neighbors'). You can get a decent lopper for about $30.

## DIGGING TOOLS

Still in the essentials, you need a spade or shovel (unless you're a rooftop gardener and never dig in the earth). The classic shovel is for digging. Buy a good quality one that won't break when you do something dumb like pry a boulder out with it. Of course, now you say you wouldn't do anything like that—but you will. You can buy a decent shovel at the hardware store for $15 and up. A rubber coating at the end of the handle may help prevent blisters. A spade has a flat spade. I like my "border" spade a lot. It cost about $50, and I'll probably have it forever. I mainly use it for dividing: once you've dug up a big clump of daylilies or whatever, a good thrust with the blade will cut it cleanly in half. For people of petite stature, try a lady's spade, which is a smaller version, or a border spade, which is pretty much the same thing. I like this tool for working in tight quarters to dig holes for bulbs or new perennials.

I also get good use from my digging fork. It looks a bit like a pitchfork, but has longer, thinner tines and is much lighter. A digging fork is a sturdy tool, usually with four or five steel tines that are designed to loosen a vegetable garden's soil before planting or to lift clumps of perennials for transplanting or dividing. A cheap version of this tool will bend when confronted by heavy, wet soil, hidden rocks or debris, or a really entrenched shrub rose that you've decided to move. So do invest in a better tool that will stand the test of time.

Since we're still discussing digging tools, I'd also spring for a good-quality trowel. Essentially a miniature, hand-held spade, a trowel is designed for digging small holes for things like perennials and annuals. A good strong handle and sturdy blade are necessary. You'll bend a cheap one in two days. The point of contention is where the handle meets the blade. If this isn't securely joined, it will fall apart. One-piece forged pieces of stainless steel get around this problem. Be prepared to pay at least $25 for a good trowel.

I occasionally use my dibble, which is a quaint tool for making uniform holes for seeds or small bulbs. It's essentially a pointed, plump piece of wood (like a swollen wooden carrot) that you can probably live without. But it does look picturesque on the potting bench. Speaking of which, do you need a proper potting bench? I admire the really nice ones immensely, with their stainless-steel tops and compartments for potting soil and stuff. I usually do my seeding on the dining table or kitchen floor and I plant my containers in place on the patio or balcony. Still, a potting bench would look really stylish in my sunroom.

## RAKES

Most people rake more than I do; I lack the obsession to remove every leaf and blade of grass that falls. When I had a lawn, I used a mulching mower (which I highly recommend) to chop up the leaves in my last fall mowing. I leave most leaves where they fall in the garden itself to protect plants and disintegrate over the winter. This is a judgment call, because too many leaves can compact into a slimy mess that smothers rather than protects your plants. But

**Even when its days of service are over, a leaky wheelbarrow positioned by the tool shed holds a bevy of beautiful daylilies, liatris, and 'Moonbeam' coreopsis.**

to the subject of rakes: a lightweight, aluminum leaf rake is pretty much indispensable around your property (you can get back-saving ergonomic models, as you can with many kinds of tools as well as those for lefties). Even better for working among plants in fall or spring is a rake with rubber tines that won't tear up your perennials. A small hand rake really comes in handy for tight spots.

A heavy iron garden rake gets most of its use in the vegetable garden for leveling and smoothing after digging. I often turn the head upside down to get rid of dirt clods by beating them with it. I'm not kidding; it's the best way.

## HOES

Not everyone needs a hoe. I use a standard type, mainly for making furrows for planting seeds of corn, beans, and other vegetables. I used to have an old hoe that must have been in the garage when I bought the house. Poorly designed and constructed, the blade would occasionally fly off the handle. I was doing some serious weeding one day, chopping out clumps of grass and clover, when the flying-off-the-handle episodes became more frequent and dangerous.

**Few things in gardening cause as much cussing as a hose that kinks.**

So get a quality hoe that will stay in one piece. Another hoe I use more frequently is the "action" or "shuffle" hoe, which has a thin sharp blade on a hollow head that shuffles back and forth, and which cuts small weeds off just below the soil surface.

## HOSES AND GARDEN MISCELLANY

Even if you put in an automated underground irrigation system, you'll still need a hose. Few things in gardening cause as much cussing as a hose that kinks. You'll pay more for a quality hose, but, again, you'll keep your cool. Get one longer than you think you'll need. A 50' hose is shorter than you imagined.

Among the things I use on a constant basis are plastic spray bottles (for soap sprays), a plastic ten-gallon bucket for toting tools and collecting garden debris, a hose reel for quick roll-ups, and various hose attachments. For container gardening, I use a watering wand with an adjustable head that I can dial up to get everything from a fine mist to a powerful jet. It's similar to the one you may have in your shower that pulses and massages. The advantage is that you can get a delicate spray so that you don't wash away seedlings, or a more aggressive spray for washing down the patio and everything in between.

Among the tools I've yet to find a use for are the hand claw (I don't think my plants would want me disturbing their roots on a daily basis) and the bulb planter, an aluminum tube that would be better for taking geological core samples if it weren't guaranteed to bring on carpal tunnel syndrome within three minutes of use. Surely I've had a few others that have long been buried in the back corners of the potting shed.

Once your relatives and friends see that you've become a gardener, you're bound to get garden stuff as gifts. If they garden, perhaps they'll give you useful things like pots and tools. Try to steer them in the right direction so that they don't give you trinkets like pink flamingos and resin plaques that say "My Garden" or "Squirrel Crossing."

# ■ Start to Plant!

At some point you'll need to stop reading, quit planning, and go buy some plants. Get yourself to your local nursery. Ask for help. Try not to get distracted by every pretty flower you see. Follow your list just like at the grocery store. There are plenty of suggestions within the regional section of this book, which immediately follows this introduction.

Part of being a good gardener is being a good observer. Watch what happens in your garden through the seasons and learn from it. As your thumb starts to get a little green glow, branch out and try new things. If you do indeed kill a plant (and you will), figure out why. Plants want to live, so something went wrong. The answer is usually that the plant received too much or too little water. Always poke your finger in the soil several inches deep before you water. If it's moist, hold off.

You're off and running. Take some classes. Read some more books. Get dirty.

# 🌸 Section 2

# Your Rocky Mountain Garden

## ■ Ground Level

### IMPROVING ON NATURE

**M**ost people don't give soil a second thought. It's there beneath their green lawn, of course, their kids and dogs track it onto the carpets, and they wash it off their cars every few weeks. It's dirt and it's something to combat. Gardeners call it soil and they don't get so uptight about it. I've spent most of my life with my hands in the soil, getting dirty. To me, soil is a wondrous thing. Little more than bits of rock worn down by water and wind into tiny particles over eons, it makes life on Earth possible. That which springs from the earth eventually dies and returns to it, enriching and renewing it, making more life possible. I think "dust to dust" says it more succinctly, but it misses the idea of renewal.

Your soil is the culmination of the past hundred thousand years or so of life in it. It may be the remnants of an ancient mountain long scoured from the earth or a primeval sea now raised up. Rivers or glaciers may have deposited it on the site where you now live (most parts of the Rocky Mountain region were heavily glaciated during the last ice age). Your soil is the

---

*A high-altitude floral tapestry includes coral bells,
Shirley poppies, pansies, and pink dianthus.*

product of all the plants and animals that have lived on and in it. Perhaps more recently, settlers plowed it to plant wheat or corn. Perhaps a family tended tomatoes and cabbage there not so long ago. Perhaps bulldozers and other heavy equipment rampaged over it only recently as carpenters constructed your home. If so, your soil might not seem so wondrous.

Having lived and gardened in this region most of my life, I've encountered several different sorts of soil. For the last two of my homes, I've dug a couple spadefuls of earth before I sealed the deal. I just like to know what I'm getting into. I've overlooked groaning pipes, sagging gutters, and deplorable shag carpeting—but I want the lowdown on the dirt. Not that I want to change it—far from it—but I want to know what's possible.

There's a prevailing attitude in gardening that whatever sort of soil you have, it's not good enough. Good enough for what? It's only deficient if you wish to grow plants in it that didn't evolve in it or soil similar to it. Our idea of "good" soil tends to be the kind that grows gardens out of picture books, full of roses and delphiniums, or perhaps corn as high as an elephant and watermelons the size of, well, watermelons. Different kinds of soil support different kinds of plants. Before you declare your soil "bad" and undertake to "improve" it, consider what kind of plant life it will support. If you jump the gun and decide to alter your soil to support picture-book plants, you may deny yourself the opportunity to grow the thousands of native and adaptable plants from similar regions around the world ideally suited to the conditions that already exist beneath your feet.

As I've traveled around the Rocky Mountain West over the past 20 or so years as a professional horticulturist, the first topic of conversation with gardeners is always soil. In Salt Lake City, Boise, Billings, Casper, Cheyenne, Lincoln, Fargo, Fort Collins, Grand Junction, and Steamboat Springs, gardeners dish their dirt. It doesn't hold water. It's too sticky. It doesn't drain. It's rocky. It's hard to dig. It's always something. Someone once told me that one of the secrets of happiness wasn't having what you want, but wanting what you have. The happiest gardeners I know (and gardeners are usually a pretty happy bunch) have made peace with their soil. They know exactly what it's capable of growing and explore all the zillions of plants that thrive in that type of soil.

Having said that, there's no need to forego the flowers and vegetables you've dreamt about growing all your life. You shouldn't have to move to Portland to grow roses or to Seattle to grow lilies. You may need to relocate to a warmer clime if you have your heart set on palms and bougainvilleas—or do you? There's always container gardening, as we've mentioned before and will return to later. I've said before, almost everything is possible one way or another. Even without great expense, you can create an area conducive to growing roses, tomatoes, or whatever you simply must have. Here's what you need to know.

Soils in the West fall into two main groups: clay and sand. Clay soil is predominant (it's the number-one soil across the world), with very small soil particles and an insignificant amount of organic matter, such as the debris of leaves and wood. In addition, it likely measures as alkaline on the pH scale, which of itself is no big deal unless it's so alkaline that it's off the charts. Our water in the West is alkaline too. This only affects the survival and growth of plants that absolutely must have acidic soil to succeed, such as heaths, heathers, azaleas, rhododendrons, mountain laurels, blueberries, and hollies. Surely you can manage without these seven plants. (A number of pretty woodland flowers from heavily forested parts of the country, such as trilliums, are probably out of the question here, but they're hard to grow even in their home states.)

**Clay soil amended with organic matter supports a bounty of vegetables and herbs.**

So suppose you want a super vegetable garden or perhaps a row of hybrid tea roses. The heaviest, stickiest clay soil won't support them; but moderate clay will, as long as you don't overwater and drown them. Too much water is just as bad or worse than too little. Clay soil, because of its tiny particles, sticks together when wet and drains slowly. Plant roots need oxygen but can't get it when the spaces between the particles are filled with water. Heavy clay soil may remain moist as long as two months after a heavy rainstorm. Plants subjected by the gardener to way too much "rain" eventually rot and die. I used to drive by a home in an area of town I knew had pretty heavy clay soil. The homeowners planted a big Austrian pine, staked the heck out of it, made a big dike around it, and proceeded to water it as if it were a Christmas tree next to the hearth. It died. They replaced it the next spring. And the next. And the next. I finally changed the route I took; I wonder if they have. Some gardeners complain about the high cost of annuals, but surely a 20' pine must be the most expensive.

The fact that clay soil holds water for an extended time (it even crusts over to help seal in moisture) has resulted in the vast array of wildflowers that inhabit our mountains, plains, and plateaus. They generally sink their roots deep, enabling them to ride out periods of drought and cold weather. They wedge their roots between and under rocks, the better to soak up heat or to explore for moisture below. Many, perhaps most, have evolved on a mineral-rich, hubris-low diet. The natural environment for these lovely natives offers little organic matter. When grown in rich soil, with too much water, they often rot and die.

There's a reason why you don't see our beautiful penstemons much outside our region. In areas with vast groves of deciduous trees, such as New England, the soil is the product of leaves falling each autumn for many thousands of years, breaking down into organically rich soil. In the West, where native trees are limited to just a few, such as aspen, cottonwood, and scrub oak, the soil is more ex-rock than ex-tree. The exception, of course, is where evergreens grow and their needles have become an important component of the soil. This is also where, by the way, you may have an acidic soil due to these needles' breakdown—meaning that perhaps a rhododendron is not entirely out of the question. (Even in alkaline Denver, beneath century-old blue spruce, the soil has become sufficiently acidic for some tough species of rhododendrons to prosper.) But back to our natives: Those accustomed to an organically lean diet can't cope with the riches gardeners customarily heap upon their soils.

Sandy soil is composed of much larger particles than clay soil. Water drains through it quickly and, like clay, this type of soil doesn't contain much organic matter. If you live in a sandy soil area, perhaps you're near a river (or perhaps an ancient one), where rushing spring waters deposited the particles picked up as they overflowed their normal banks. Or perhaps, during the last ice age, as glaciers chugged slowly down valleys, they didn't scrape off the high terrain where you now sit. This is the case in my garden.

The time-honored way of producing "good" soil (from clay or sand) is to add a layer of organic matter, about 1" to 2", and spade or till it in. Manure and compost are the most common materials. Peat moss used to be recommended as well, before we knew how fast the nonrenewable peat bogs of the world were disappearing just to pamper our roses. (Peat moss is an important element in soil mixtures formulated for potted plants because it inhibits the growth of bacteria and fungus, which prey on and kill seedlings. Peat moss is nature's form of fungicide, but should be used wisely and sparingly.) If you decide to enrich part of your garden with organic matter, such as a vegetable area, adding manure or compost is a good way.

You can also grow a "cover crop" of rye grass, sown in fall, and then tilled into the ground in spring. You can also dig in coarse materials such as leaves and straw. They'll break down quickly with the help of earthworms and microbes present in the soil. The result will be what's called a more "friable" soil, meaning that it's looser. The ultimate in friable soil comes in a bag. Reach into a bag of store-bought potting soil and you'll feel the ideal growing medium for great tomatoes and super lilies. It's organically rich and drains well, but holds moisture at the same time. "Eureka!" you might think, "I'll just cover my ground with an inch or two of potting soil, till it in, and I'll be set to go." People with more money than brains have tried this approach—with mixed results. For starters, this soil is a bit too light and it blows away. It's also beyond most of our means.

The most reasonable approach for modifying soil for special groups of plants—or for cases where builders have trampled the life out of the soil that was there—is either to add organic matter or haul in topsoil. There's no shame in buying dirt. Check it out first. Feel it, smell it, try to roll it into a ball. Ask gardening friends what they think of it. Make sure what's delivered is exactly from the source you checked.

Your soil changes as you work in it. Roots delve down and aerate it. So do earthworms. So do you as you dig and till it. Stems and leaves fall through the seasons and return to the soil. Everything you do in the garden affects it, even walking on it. Avoid doing that since it compresses and compacts the life out of it (although not quite as efficiently as a bulldozer), leaving it starved for oxygen. Every gardener has to get into his or her beds and borders for weeding and deadheading, but tread lightly. Especially avoid trudging around in the garden when it's wet or you'll end up with soil the consistency of the clods you scrape off your boots. Make paths in areas to which you need routine access, such as vegetable areas and flowerbeds for cutting. We'll talk more about that later.

## THE JOY OF COMPOSTING

In the meantime, value not just the living parts of your garden, but the dead ones. Use the garden debris to enrich the soil in areas you want to improve. Composting can be rather casual or become somewhat of a compulsion. There are books written on the subject, and if you become infatuated with compost, get one of them to make your composting experience all that it can be. But maybe you should start nonchalantly. The casual way (which I practice) is to let some things compost in place—such as fallen leaves—as long as they don't smother what's under them. In spring, the biggest chunks get raked up and added to a loose pile made up of other leaves, thin stems, celery tops, and over-the-hill lettuce from the kitchen. Poinsettias from last Christmas and African violets that bit the dust are in there too. Once in a while, about two times in the season, I get an enormous burst of enthusiasm and tear up my pile. I put the good, black, crumbly stuff at the bottom in buckets and toss the pile back together like a salad. I add the compost to potting soil and top-dress vegetables with it.

## THE CASE FOR TOPDRESSING V. MULCHING

This brings us to mulching. That sentence may sound like the most boring one you've ever read, but I encourage you to read on or you'll be sorry. Now I'm threatening. More harm has come to gardens in the name of mulching than you might imagine. I wish the word "mulch" could be replaced in our vocabularies by topdressing, so that we would understand that it must be renewed to be effective. Mulching has its place, but not in my garden. Let's draw the distinction between topdressing and mulching. As I said, I topdress vegetables, perennials, bulbs, and shrubs such as peonies, roses, and lilies. That black, crumbly stuff that I pull out from the bottom of the compost pile is pure organic matter full of fiber and nutrients. As time and earthworms work it down into the soil, it both feeds and improves the "tilth" of the soil.

Farmers talk a lot about tilth. It's essentially the way the soil looks and feels, and for a farmer, good tilth means just the right blend of coarse and fine particles for plowing and hoeing. The right tilth for corn may not be ideal for columbines. As you work in your soil from season to season and learn how it feels, and you see the results of the plants, you'll begin to get a sense of what kind of soil grows what kinds of plants best. Cooks learn the same kind of lessons from their pancake batters and bread doughs. Words can't explain just exactly how perfect pancake batter pours (and judging from my pancakes, I certainly can't). But I do know dirt. My experience has helped me judge what might want to grow in it, or what it might need for something else to grow in it.

Topdressing with homemade compost is the best thing you can do for traditional plants that like nutritious, organically rich soil. Do it year after year—perhaps in both spring and fall—and your soil will become even better at supporting and sustaining those plants. Topdressing also helps to conserve moisture, since you are adding a barrier between the soil and the air. Now all this sounds pretty much like what you know about mulching. Topdressing and mulching are about the same except that mulching has gotten completely out of hand. What sounds good for the garden has turned into an entrenched custom that can actually be detrimental.

I blame bark nuggets. They're the lazy person's way to make a landscape look "finished." The idea is that the bark creates a layer between the soil and air, conserving moisture and suppressing weeds. The trouble is that, as a mulch, bark doesn't cut it. An organic mulch's job is to break down and enrich the soil. I've seen bark nuggets older than me. They break down very slowly in our climate (no worm is going to tackle one of those) and the microorganisms that do help them decompose require lots of nitrogen. The bark nuggets steal this nutrient from your plants. I've seen plantings virtually buried in bark where the plants haven't grow discernibly in five years.  I even get annoyed when we have really big rainstorms and the street gutters flood over their levels. The water picks up a load of bark, floats it down the street to my garden, and deposits it on top of my ice plants and moss roses. The only use I have for the nuggets is chucking them at squirrels.

Worse yet, people often lay plastic or weed-barrier fabrics beneath the nuggets. When this is done, oxygen has a hard time getting in. Earthworms and other life forms die. What was once a thriving ecosystem ceases to exist. For all intents and purposes, the soil is dead. Dust blows in amidst the bark, and within a few years, weeds take root. Nature always finds a way. If this sounds pretty grim, it is. Bark may be natural, but it's not natural to spread it around plants. There's not a single ecosystem on earth where the trees all shed their bark and spread it evenly on the ground. Don't even get me started on the bark they dye as red as Lucy's hair.

So what sorts of mulches are effective and appropriate?  Any sort of organic compost is appropriate, where needed, to nourish plants, conserve moisture, and suppress weed seedlings.

**Small gravel makes an effective mulch for early blooming grape hyacinth and miniature yellow iris.**

There's one more form of mulch that I do recommend: gravel. I'm not talking about river rock or that horrid white quartz with which my mother once decided to surround our patio for reasons known only to her. Small, pleasant pea gravel makes excellent mulch for the plants that like it. A mulch of this type is often incorporated with the use of rocks whether you're a rock gardener or not, but especially if you are. It does look tidy and finished, even if those words are barely in my gardening vocabulary.

Many plants have evolved in stony ground where the surface has a scree of small, loose gravel. This inorganic mulch helps the soil below both to stay cool and evaporate less. It also keeps the crowns of plants (the area where the stems meet soil) high and dry and prevents rot in unseasonably wet weather. You'll find gravel works in many parts of the Rocky Mountain West, especially in plateaus and in the Great Basin as well as in many other semiarid lands around the world. Plants that can benefit from a mulch of pea gravel include hardy cactus, agaves, yuccas, penstemons, and many others.

Moisture-loving alpine plants—the traditional inhabitants of rock gardens—prosper in free-draining soil with a gravel mulch to help keep the soil evenly moist. Rock gardeners on the plains and plateaus, where summer temperatures soar and humidity drops, often concentrate on native and adaptable plants of small stature that can withstand harsh, dry environments, rather than the true alpine flora found above timberline, where it's always cool and moist. Edelweiss balks at growing in dry, dusty Denver. But gardeners in the foothills and mountains fare much better with this tiny alpine jewel that makes rock gardening so rewarding. I grew edelweiss for several years and, at the risk of offending the legions of *The Sound of Music* fans, it's not so special. The flowers, regardless of what the song says, are the color of really old (formerly) white sheets. I never

**Purple pasque flowers and 'Stresa' tulips benefit from a sunny exposure in a rock garden on the plains.**

felt the slightest urge to burst into song. Then a really hot summer came along and the "blossom of snow" bit the dust. One way to keep alpine plants relatively satisfied in a hostile environment is to position them on the north-facing side of your rock garden outcroppings. They'll stay cooler and more protected from drying winds and can wedge their roots deep into the crevices.

## WATER, HE WROTE

Periodic water shortages appear to be likely in the West for the foreseeable future. A garden that can get by on less water seems only logical. Making the most of what we have is the spirit of gardeners in our region. You can be a water-smart gardener in many ways.

For starters, reduce turf areas to manageable sizes. Water them both deeply and infrequently. Keep that mower blade set to the highest level; long grass shades itself and keeps the soil temperature down. A lawn sheared putting-green short may register as hot as an asphalt parking lot in midsummer. During periods of water restrictions, the ordinances often dictate that you water either early in the morning or later in the evening. This is a good practice to adopt regardless of whether restrictions are in effect. When watering in the heat of the day, you lose more moisture to evaporation.

Unfortunately, watering restrictions often dictate that you water for a short time only, such as 10 or 15 minutes. This doesn't take into account what your hose's pressure and flow rate is, what sort of soil you're on, or for that matter, what types of plants you're watering. Clay soils will obviously hold moisture better and longer, but short-interval watering is problematical. You might as well spit on your lawn for as much good as a short burst from the sprinkler will accomplish. It will only moisten the top of the soil, tempting roots to come to the surface, where they're more vulnerable to the dessicating winds and unrelenting rays of the sun. If you have a choice, "save up" your allotted water and apply it all at once so it sinks in and encourages roots to delve deeply and stay there. Deep-root watering is advisable for trees and shrubs during extended rainless periods. You can purchase a hose attachment that you plunge a foot or so into the earth every few feet around the dripline of the trees (the outer extent of their canopies) where the bulk of their roots reside.

Although I don't think they work well for perennial borders, drip systems or "leaky hoses" may be an ideal way to make the most of your water in vegetable and cutting gardens. They work well in raised beds that you may have filled with loose, friable soil suitable for great vegetable growth. Emitters can also be rigged to containers, leaving you carefree if you take off for vacation and don't trust your friend or neighbor to be as attentive to your plants as you are. Do-it-yourselfers can buy everything they need at hardware or building supply stores to rig up low-cost effective systems.

You can also go low tech. My vegetable garden is planted the way that Native Americans in the Southwest used to grow crops. They used so-called "waffle" patterns, with corn and peppers planted in depressed areas between short earthen walls. Rainfall fills the depressions; water can be periodically added to keep the plants growing. I simply turn on the hose for a few minutes and let it fill up the waffles, and I need to do this only once a week during hot weather.

Xeriscaping is the practice of water-wise gardening. One of the principles of xeriscaping is to group plants by need. It's a practical, no-nonsense approach. Put plants with high irrigation requirements in one bed. That way you can do a little pampering. Periods of drought shouldn't mean that you have to say goodbye to cherished plants. Topdress them with water-retentive compost, create earthen dikes around them to collect rain when it falls, and think of them as you work around the house. I save water from household uses for the few plants I pamper. When I'm warming up the shower water, I put a bucket in the tub to save the first few gallons before the water gets hot. I save the water when I change the pets' water bowls or when I rinse fruits and vegetables in the sink. Some municipalities have strict regulations about reusing "gray" household water for watering plants, so check with your local water provider before you siphon your bathwater for the rose garden.

## FEAST OR FAMINE?

Fertilizer companies spend lots of money trying to convince you to buy their products to feed your plants. Their packages show off big, bright marigolds and enormous, mouthwatering vegetables, making it seem like a good idea to shovel on the fertilizer to get these results. In truth, there are several ways to supply the nutrients that your plants need and there are plants that don't need or want any extra food. A compelling argument can be made that amending and topdressing your soil with organic matter supplies all the nutrients your plants should need (and that the natives and adaptables don't even need that). As far as most perennials, shrubs, and trees go, this principle is exactly what I follow. The only exceptions I make are for roses and first-year plants, where I want to encourage more vigorous root activity. But the commercials play heavily in our minds and we're tempted to go for bigger daisies and taller delphiniums.

We get them with too much fertilizer, as the plants grow fast and furiously until the garden is a heavy mass of flopping flowers held up by our feeble attempts at staking. This house of cards needs only a stiff breeze to come crashing down. Lean and mean is the way to go, keeping additional applications of nitrogen (the main culprit in overblown growth) to a minimum. Steady, even, sustainable growth and size should be your goal, unless you intend to compete in giant vegetable contests.

There are a number of plants that may grow best with some additional kinds of feeding. Aside from competition-sized pumpkins, these include annuals, container plants, normal vegetables, and a few oddballs with particular dietary requirements, such as rhododendrons and tomatoes.

## FEEDING TIME

Let's face it: the length of our growing season is shorter in the Rocky Mountain West than in most parts of the country. Mountain gardeners are acutely aware of this; but even on the plains and plateaus, we're only truly safe from frost in July and August. So we want results. Fast. I've got lots of boxes of fertilizer in my potting shed that I use sequentially throughout the growing season. In April and May, I feed a water-soluble, high-nitrogen fertilizer (such as Miracle-Gro or Schultz) to cool-season vegetables (such as lettuce and spinach), cool-season annuals (such as snapdragons and pansies), and seedlings still inside. Tulips, daffodils, and other bulbs

### TO FEED OR NOT TO FEED

**WATCH THE NITRO!** Like many of our native perennials that don't need or want supplemental nitrogen, many annuals don't require it either. Receiving too much beyond what they extract from the soil will send them into a super growth spurt that will result in jungle-like foliage but few if any flowers. This list includes nasturtiums, moss roses, cosmos, moon vines, morning glories, California poppies, bachelor buttons, and larkspurs.

**SIX-PACK SECRETS.** One of the secrets of the nursery industry is that six-pack annuals have all usually been treated with a growth retardant that dwarfs them and forces the plants to poke out their first flowers prematurely (color sells). The effect of this retardant lingers like a hangover and requires heavy feeding to overcome it. This applies to almost all common annuals, including salvias, sweet alyssum, flowering tobacco, marigolds, trailing verbenas, impatiens, petunias, gomphrena, straw flowers, and statice. It's always a good idea to give annuals a shot of diluted, water-soluble fertilizer at planting time. It helps to prevent transplant shock and gets the roots off to a good start. There are also commercial products available that contain vitamin B-1 to help prevent shock. Some gardeners crush some of their own B-1, mix it in water, and use it the same way with good results.

**TOUGH MOVES.** Transplanting can be traumatic. It's the equivalent of moving to a new house and throwing a dinner party that night. It's difficult for the plant to both put down roots and support all that top growth and all those flowers. To help the annuals cope, I pinch off those first flowers and the growth tips. This helps the roots settle in, as well as promotes bushiness. It might pain you to remove the very flowers you bought these plants for, but with proper feeding and water, you'll be rewarded with at least double the flowers you would have gotten had you not pinched them. ■

get a shot of super phosphate while they're actively growing to plump up the bulbs for the next season. Roses get a handful of granular fertilizer formulated especially for them, scratched into the soil at their bases.

In late May and June, newly planted perennials, shrubs, annuals (see sidebar on page 75), vegetables, and container plants get shots of high nitrogen every 10 days until July. Tomatoes get fed at planting time with a slow-release fertilizer, as well as fertilizer especially formulated for them, every 10 days. Container plants also get slow-release fertilizer (such as Osmocote) worked into the soil at planting time. Starting in July, I stop fertilizing new perennials and shrubs. I switch from a high-nitrogen fertilizer to a "bloom booster" that contains a higher ratio of potassium and phosphate as compared to nitrogen. This formula is delivered every 7 to 10 days to annuals and container plants, and vegetables get fed with a similar formula made for them. This goes on until late August, when I get really lazy. If it looks like summer might linger, I continue feeding container plants until frost hits. I also have special fertilizers and supplements for indoor plants such as African violets and orchids. For whatever you choose to grow, there are options you can pursue to achieve success. Getting to know the experts at your local garden center, public garden, or county extension office may help you with specific concerns about formulations for specific plant types or local conditions.

# ■ Design for Living

We live in a region of great beauty and diversity. Vast, windswept plains meet pine-dotted foothills. The hills give way to awe-inspiring peaks and ridges with valleys nestled between them. Great high plateaus separate the mountain chains. Mountain streams drain the mountains, converging into rivers that carve through canyons and gorges, emptying into mighty lakes or continuing their voyage to the sea.

Upon this beautiful land, to which most of our ancestors have come only recently, towns and cities have been built. As people have moved to our region from other parts of the country and around the world, their cultures have met and mixed, intermingling with those of the Native Americans. Explorers and settlers left their names and legacies in our towns, mountains, and bodies of water, from Cortez to Pikes Peak to Clark Fork. Some of our great-great-grandparents, perhaps from Russia or Germany, broke the sod to grow wheat, onions, and beets. Others from Japan and Italy grew produce and planted orchards. Native peoples of the Southwest grew corn and chili, and our Spanish and Mexican ancestors continued that tradition.

This intermingling of cultures is our regional gardening heritage. Our gardens reflect elements from diverse sources, as well as an appreciation of the natural landscape. As I've visited gardens throughout the Rocky Mountain West, I'm continually surprised and delighted by the spirit, creativity, and tenacity of its gardeners and their deep respect for the land. I've lived and gardened here for most of my life and I count myself lucky. In no other region are there so many opportunities to grow an almost infinite variety of plants. Settlers first brought seeds and cuttings to our region in covered wagons (they often stuck cuttings of roses, apple trees, and lilacs in potatoes to keep them fresh during the journey). Many of those tough pioneer plants continue to beautify our gardens. Each culture has contributed favorite perennials, annuals, vegetables, and herbs to the plant palette from which we can select. Add to that our array of lovely native wildflowers, and that should be enough to keep any gardener occupied for a lifetime. New introductions from areas around the world with similar climates continue to become available to us, such as Russian sage, South African ice plant, and Turkish veronica.

The designs of our gardens may draw upon influences as far-flung as the origins of our plants. The concept of a sun-drenched courtyard with splashing fountain comes to us from the Mediterranean region, especially from Spain and Morocco, along with classical Italian ideas. French and Dutch formality figure in our use of clipped hedges and topiary, alleys of trees, and reflecting pools. The Japanese respect for the elements of water, wood, and stone translates beautifully into the Rocky Mountain landscape. From Mexico, we inherit some of the brightest and boldest flowers in our gardens, including zinnias, marigolds, and dahlias as well as the idea of using vivid colors fearlessly. Many of our other brilliant flowers originated in South America, Africa, India, Australia, and the South Seas. From the English, Scottish, and Irish come most of our concepts of how to display a flower garden, from the sophisticated perennial border to the "anything goes" cottage garden.

As you create your garden, you'll likely draw on inspirations from many sources. More formal elements may be more prominent "in town," and more naturalistic designs common to rural areas. That's not always the case. I know a lovely manicured herb garden set at a country home and several wild meadows in the heart of the city. The architecture of your home may suggest the best way to go, but your own sensibilities should really be your driving force. Do anything you please. It's your garden and you're the one who lives with it. I'm happy if you heed my advice; I'd probably be better off if I heeded it as well. My garden is a smorgasbord of all the plants and ideas I like. The borders are borrowed from the Brits, but populated by native plants and heirlooms. The picket fence would look at home in New England. My patio and balconies, with their red umbrellas and "explosion-in-a-paint-factory" color scheme, draw elements from Mexican bazaars, southern verandas, and Californian bungalows. My herb and vegetable garden, with its waffle pattern of irrigation, owes much to the Native Americans of the Southwest. Your new garden may pay homage to memories of your Aunt Martha's garden, a trip to Hawaii, or a great love of Italian cuisine.

Whatever you create, give it a Rocky Mountain twist. Incorporate ornamental grasses to bend and rustle in the wind, as they do on the plains. Perhaps a backdrop of blue spruce will provide a cooling influence on the hot-colored flowers of summer. In winter, the tree can twinkle with a wrapping of holiday lights. Cherish the wildflowers that perform best in your locality, from high altitude columbines to dryland yuccas. Honor the plants that our grandparents cherished, from fragrant sweet Williams, sweet peas, and lilacs to picturesque hollyhocks, lilies, and bellflowers.

Add a water feature to trickle and splash, reflect our gorgeous blue sky, and provide for the birds. Find a spot for a nesting box or birdhouse so your family can watch an avian family from building their nest to the first flight of the chicks. Use indigenous stone and rocks for paths, retaining walls, and as plant habitat. Celebrate our cultural diversity with pots made in Mexico, Italy, or Malaysia. Find furniture for your outdoor living room that reflects the architecture of your home, whether it's a Victorian painted lady, adobe hacienda, Midwest farmhouse, or a mountain log home. Make a garden that reflects all the joy and beauty of living in the Rocky Mountain West.

**LEFT: Iceland poppy petals glow like stained glass and are backed by red barberry foliage.**
**RIGHT: The sweeping curves of a mountain border teem with sweet William, pansies, and poppies.**

## BORDER BASICS

Perhaps more words have been written about making borders than any other single subject in horticulture. It's an endlessly fascinating subject because each border is different. Each is like a living, growing painting. Here's a no-fuss approach to simplify the process of creating a beautiful border.

Create the boundary first. This will be partially suggested by the length of a fence, wall, or house. Whatever you do, make the depth of the border much deeper than you think is necessary—at least 5' or 6'. Eight feet is even better. A narrow strip just isn't very useful. It'll quickly be jammed with tall plants dwarfing the short ones and with no chance for a sequence of blooms throughout the season. So lay it out, till it, and add organic matter if you're going for traditional perennials and shrubs such as roses, peonies, daisies, daylilies, and the like. For natives and adaptables that don't want or need organic matter, just break up the soil and rake it smooth.

Armed with a list based on what colors you like and plants you know you want, head to the nursery. Stick to your color scheme, such as blue, pink, and white with silver foliage accents, or orange, yellow, and purple with chartreuse foliage accents. I always recommend buying the smallest-sized pot available, both for saving money and for the ease of transplanting them. Make sure all the plants you combine in your new border share the same water and sun requirements. Buy short, medium, and tall. Get shrubs and ornamental grasses. Look for early, middle, and late bloomers. Take time to look at the leaves both for color and shape, some big and some small. Stay aware of the shapes of plants as well. Some should be spiky, others round, others creeping. Even if a particular plant may not hold great appeal standing alone, it may look smashing when you pair it with another of contrasting color, shape, or texture. A red barberry bush might not catch your eye right off the bat, but imagine it with brilliant poppies in front. Not every flower in the garden can be a star; some just make the stars look even more glamorous. Small-flowered perennials such as baby's breath, lavender, lady's mantle (*Alchemilla*), apple blossom grass (*Gaura*), and snow daisy may be pretty little things, but they combine gloriously with high-power roses, hollyhocks, red-hot pokers, lilies, and daylilies. The pairings make each plant even more striking than it is on its own.

When you bring your purchases home, lay them out in the border. Knowing that the tags are usually a bit optimistic about height and spread, move the plants around as you please, tall things in the back, short in the front. See how the grassy foliage of daylilies looks with a mound of fine-textured catmint in front (and imagine how the yellow daylilies pair with the blue catmint). After you've laid it all out, go away. Have a beer or go fix dinner. Come back later, even the next day, and see what you think. Mix it back up. Leave a few blank spaces to integrate annuals, herbs, and even vegetables if you like. As long as your spacing is reasonable (that daisy isn't going to cover 3' no matter how long you live), your border will grow and thrive because of you and despite you. Just add water and a bit of fertilizer the first season and your adventure is on. As the border matures (and you mature as a gardener), you'll add and edit. Unlike a painting you must finally declare finished and sign your name to, your border is always a work in progress with your distinctive signature written all over it.

## LIVING IT UP

Residing in the Rocky Mountain West allows us to truly live outdoors for much of the year. Even on a sunny winter day, you might find me on my patio sipping tea and playing with the dogs. I've even been tempted to sleep on the balcony outside my bedroom, the better to appreciate the sweet scent of the June flowers on the linden tree next to it. I just haven't found the right sort of outdoor bed.

As you plan your garden, give priority to where you'll spend time in it. A sunny spot is ideal in the mornings in summer, when our dry air has yet to warm up, as well as in other parts of the year. Shade is also essential during summer heat. Rarely do we experience the torrid heat common in other parts of the country, so a shady venue is nearly always pleasant.

Consider having more than one space for outdoor living. I have two patios—one in sun, the other in shade—and a little break space by the potting shed where I can hang out and enjoy the vegetable garden. The balcony overlooking the front garden is one of my favorite spots. Whenever you can devise a place such as a deck or balcony from which to view your garden from above, it gives you an entirely new and fresh perspective (and you can't be distressed by caterpillar-chewed leaves or the newly planted snapdragons through which the dogs just rampaged). Elevated living spaces can often be oriented to take in views beyond the beauty of your garden. I get just a glimpse of the mountains through the trees and a century-old tower at an amusement park about six blocks away (and on summer nights I can hear the screams of roller coaster thrill-seekers). Your neighborhood may be a bit more sedate, but even so, position your spaces where you can create a sanctuary away from the world. Although, I must point out, a lovely front porch with rocking chairs and ferns can be a nice place to see neighbors, watch joggers, and greet the mail carrier. I remember my grandparents spending hours on a porch right out of a Norman Rockwell painting. My grandfather read the paper with his dog at his feet and my grandmother shelled peas and crocheted. Maybe it's genetics—I'm destined to start doing needlework at any moment.

As I've mentioned before, an outdoor living room might work best with a sense of enclosure, whether it's a partial walls, railings, trellises, or planters. You may or may not have a view worth saving, but if you do, be very careful about what you plant near your deck or patio. Those little upright junipers will soon turn into big upright junipers that will obliterate the very scenery you moved here to enjoy.

A charming way to create a quiet destination away from phones and laundry is to construct a gazebo or pergola. Gazebos usually have a Victorian flare with a steeply pitched octagonal roof; pergolas are usually beams supported by columns on which to grow rambunctious grapes or wisteria. To my mind, a gazebo especially calls out for a skirt of flowers—especially fragrant ones—to enhance its Victorian roots. A gazebo plopped in the middle of a lawn seems as stranded as a whale on the beach.

Getting to a destination garden room requires paths. When you draw them out on paper, they may look perfectly charming and practical, but only time will tell if they work. Pets and children don't have much respect for the clever curves you've created to gently guide you to your gazebo. They will choose the most direct route. Now, you can fill up the spaces around your curving path with impenetrable roses and daylilies, and you've removed the shortcut. However you plan how to get where you're going, think both practically and romantically and then make it work.

A garden path can be the most romantic component of a garden. Strolling down a pretty one, with flowers to sniff and lavender to pinch, can be as lovely in your own garden as in any vacation spot in England. What's beneath your feet is as important as the plants on either side. The choice of materials will help create the ambience of your garden. Random red flagstone, put together like pieces of a jigsaw puzzle, is a Rocky Mountain natural. You can grow thyme, hens and chicks, and other crevice plants to fill in the seams. Brick pavers also make beautiful paths, and you can dress up a plain concrete path with brick edging. Fine gravel paths add sound to your stroll with a gentle crunch. I really like them. Gravel can also be dressed up with brick or, in a naturalistic garden, blend gracefully into the plantings and boulders. Gravel and bricks also lend themselves to pathways in vegetable, herb, rose, and cutting gardens. Precast concrete pavers can be effectively combined with brick edging to reduce costs. They look a bit too new at first but soon mellow with a bit of dirt and wear. I don't care for paths of bark nuggets because they're awkward to walk on and the bark doesn't stay where you put it, getting kicked around or floating away. I just can't find a kind word for those nuggets.

## VERTICAL ELEMENTS

Arbors and trellises add tremendously to the style of your garden. They can be freestanding or attached to the walls of your house or garage or fences. So-called privacy fences can be excessively dull garden features and can be softened by trellises festooned with roses, clematis, and morning glories. Trellises prove remarkably pretty when incorporated with a gate. It's wonderful to enter a garden beneath a garland of flowers. That's the whole point of vertical structures—to bring color and fragrance up to eye-level and even higher.

There's a style to suit every taste and type of architecture. Metal arbors and trellises are often restrained and stylish, fitting easily into a contemporary setting. Traditional wooden garden structures often give a nod to their Victorian origins. If you build your own structure or hire a carpenter, you can customize a trellis or arbor to suit your taste. I wouldn't worry about it much. If you select the right vine for your conditions, most of the structure will disappear beneath it. Just make sure it's strong and secure enough to support the weight of the plant as well as to withstand wind and snow.

Arbors and trellises can be useful as well as beautiful. Pole beans and morning glories twine up three arches in my vegetable garden. Squash and gourds also climb vigorously if given a support. Combining several types of vines on one support is a good idea, such as cream-colored honeysuckle with pink climbing roses or orange trumpet vine with purple clematis. (The latter had never occurred to me until just this moment and now I can't wait to try it on

**'Heavenly Blue' morning glories cloak an iron trellis above a pot of hen and chicks.**

my patio arbor.) Sprawling, vigorous vines such as hops, morning glory, Virginia creeper, silver lace vine, and grapes can be trained across porch railings or porch roofs that face west or south to create a cool summer awning. An obliging vine can shade any area that gets blistered by summer sun in just a season or two. It's a great solution as you wait for a tree to grow.

## SHADY DEALINGS

Unless you live in a forest, the shade in your garden comes from trees that you or someone before you planted. The urban forest is an artificial one, composed largely of trees not native to our region. As I've pointed out in our discussions of soil, the ground below the trees in our yards can't have seen much more than a hundred years of leaf drop. Given our community tidiness, it's doubtful that much of that millennium of fallen leaves was ever allowed to crumble and return to the earth. In soil-making time, that's just a blink of the eye in comparison to the soils of true woodland areas. So, despite the shade, our shade gardens are composed of the same soil as the sunny parts, almost certainly devoid of much organic matter. One of the most consistent needs of shade-loving perennials is an organically enriched soil. If you imagine a sylvan paradise of luxurious ferns, hostas, and bleeding hearts, get busy amending the soil before you plant.

As you begin, analyze the quality and duration of the shade cast by trees or buildings. Much more sun filters through the fine, lacy canopy of a honey locust than that of a thick, almost impenetrable cover of linden, catalpa, large pine, or spruce. It can be pretty dark under there.

Plants willing to grow beneath a grove of mature blue spruce are few and far between. When people ask me what to put there, I answer, "A deck." I'm serious. Why fight a losing battle? Create a lovely outdoor space, perhaps accented by pots of low-light plants normally found in the darkest corners of the house, such as philodendron, pothos, wandering Jew, and spider plant.

Trees are greedy. They've had time to send their roots into every available inch of earth for nutrients and they're at the ready to soak up every drop of moisture. If you prod around beneath many trees, you'll find the soil is often powdery dry. Even if you water regularly, trees will suck it up voraciously. Planting beneath trees presents some challenges. Whatever plants you put in this environment must be tough and aggressive just to survive. Some trees are more generous with the ground beneath them and may make life a bit easier for underplantings. With vigilance, you'll garden successfully beneath almost all deciduous trees such as crabapple, maple, oak, ash, linden, redbud, catalpa, honey locust, and many more.

As in other parts of the garden, your design for a shade garden may be formal or naturalistic. In my former garden I combined both. In a square, enclosed area on the east side of the house shaded by maples, I laid out a brick-edged circle. Within the circle there was enough sun to plant a lawn that bloomed every spring with patches of yellow, purple, and lavender snow crocus. Within the planting areas I grew ferns, hostas, lamium, maroon-leaved coral bells, goat's beard, and bleeding heart. Daffodils, Solomon's seal, wood hyacinths, and other bulbs provided bright spring colors.

In another area on the opposite side of the house, I built a square dining patio in an opening surrounded by crabapple, spruce, apple, and my very least favorite, the notorious tree-of-heaven (but that's beside the point). A pleasant, cool place to eat outdoors, it also created a spot to display pots of shade-loving plants surrounded by many other shady perennials. Shade gardening has taken a bit of a hit during the recent drought in the West. These gardens are vulnerable to water shortages, but most well-established perennials can survive with less than optimum rainfall and irrigation even if they don't look their bountiful best. Many gardeners have put plans on hold; concentrating on soil amendments that will help support the perennials they eventually place there (as well as the trees above). One alternative is establishing tough ground covers such as ivy, vinca, and snow-on-the-mountain, sometimes called bishop's weed, which are incredibly tenacious.

# FEELING FALL

Fall in the Rocky Mountain West: sometimes it lingers and other years it comes crashing down under a foot of snow. Mountain gardeners know better than to count on fall-blooming perennials. Instead, the season finale comes in the form of golden aspens and the final flowers of annuals that revel in cool weather such as flowering tobacco, pansy, lobelia, black-eyed Susan, and dusty miller.

On the plains and plateaus, summer holds sway a bit longer. Starting sometime in mid-August the fall bloomers bud and begin their late-late show. Mums and asters have become the hallmark of the season; they'll provide a much better, bushier show if you remember to shear them back a few inches in both early June and early July, which will at least double the number of flowers they'd normally supply. Also coming into bloom are perennials such as 'Autumn Joy' or 'Brilliant' sedum, with reddish flower heads over broccoli-like foliage, and pink or white Japanese anemone displaying lovely, lithe blossoms with the simplicity of just five petals. 'Goldsturm' Rudbeckia turns into a glowing mass the size of a bushel basket of black-coned daisies. Hummingbird trumpet erupts in a blaze of vermillion tubular flowers that attract hummingbirds as they migrate south from Canada. These hot colors are tempered by blue mist spiraea, a tough shrub that covers

---

# TREE TALK

Trees native to our region are quite few in number. Several species of pine and spruce inhabit the mountains and foothills, along with aspen and scrub oak. The plains are largely devoid of trees except for cottonwoods and box elder hugging creekbanks and riverbanks. That's about it. All other trees are exotic. Some adapt better than others to our soil, summer heat, and low humidity; winter cold and intense sun can cause bark to split and crack.

Unless you've just moved into a brand-new home with a yard that is a blank canvas, you probably already have trees that were planted long before you got there. I've never seen a tree I've planted in one of my gardens reach maturity. I've probably only planted a dozen or so trees in the gardens I've created where I live (although I've planted many hundreds in gardens I've designed for others). It's our responsibility to select trees that will thrive where we situate them, enhance the buildings and neighborhoods, and provide homes and food for birds.

When you select a tree, don't worry about size. A small tree will settle in more quickly than a bigger one and will catch up in size in just a few years. Choose one that will prosper in your type of soil and make sure there's enough room for it at its eventual size. I just hate to see a tree disfigured to keep its branches away from power lines and streetlamp poles. Most towns and cities regulate the kind of trees and the spacing by which you must abide when planting along the street. These rules are for safety reasons.

Spruces and pines are widely adaptable and prosper away from their foothill and mountain environments. Aspen, which thrive in disturbed soil on mountain slopes, rarely reach their full potential in hot, dry environments on the plains and plateaus. Stress often invites insects and disease. I try to talk clients out of planting them and advise them on tougher, easier-care trees that can better cope with heat and drought. Here are my top picks:

CATALPA: Noted for large, heart-shaped leaves, beautiful fragrant flowers in June followed by straight, long pods (excellent for sword-fighting like my brother and I once did as boys). Extremely drought tolerant with few if any pests. Up to 80' at maturity

CRABAPPLE: A vision in spring with masses of pink or white flowers, usually followed by edible fruit—just don't plant it near walks, driveways, or patios or you'll be fuming over the squishy mess. Up to 25' at maturity.

LINDEN: A graceful, symmetrical tree with sweetly fragrant flowers in early summer. Very drought tolerant and rarely bothered by pests. Up to 60'.

HONEY LOCUST: Low-care, drought-tolerant tree that can contend with extreme conditions such as the wind in urban high-rise canyons. Small leaves basically blow away without bother in fall. The tree produces dark brown bean pods. Up to 50'.

REDBUD: A spring stunner with beautiful cerise-pink blossoms before the leaves unfurl. Perfect as an understory tree if you're crowded for space; may do best in protected areas. Up to 20'.

GOLDEN RAIN TREE: Another charming small tree for tight spaces or as an understory tree. Bright yellow flowers are a spring highlight. Best with some protection. Somewhat drought tolerant. Up to 20'.

ASH: A tough, dependable, and colorful street or lawn tree. Relatively fast growing, drought tolerant, and virtually pest and disease free. 'Autumn Purple' is especially desirable. Up to 60'.

itself in true-blue little blossoms until fall. Apple blossom grass (*Gaura lindheimeri*), sometimes known as whirling butterflies, saves its best show for the end of the season with myriad pink-tinted white flowers (like tiny apple blossoms) held on graceful arching stems.

Annuals continue their shows as well, resulting in a crescendo effect with perennials and fall foliage. Black-eyed Susans, verbenas, petunias, lantana, and many others may even seem to step up the pace as nights become cooler and longer, sensing that there's not much time left to set seeds. One of my favorite parts of fall is the surprise appearance of autumn-flowering crocus and meadow saffron (*Colchicum*). These spring-like bulbs seem to belie the calendar. Some varieties of iris also rebloom in fall. I'm still not quite used to this repeat performance and I'm startled when their lovely flowers unfurl "out of season."

All of these flowers combine stunningly with ornamental grasses in their prime. The blades of some such as switch grass turn red and gold, whereas others such as maiden grass burnish their feathery seedheads like peacocks. 'Karl Forster' reed grass stands bolt upright with its 3' honey-gold stems and heads. Ponytail grass turns from chartreuse to platinum blond like Cousin It after too much time in the swimming pool—definitely in need of a scrunchy. Fall is the reason we grow ornamental grasses. So many have come into the market that they can't all be described here. Check with your local nursery for the ones best suited to your area, but don't wait until fall. Most grasses thrive best when planted in spring, the better to develop their root systems. Late-planted grasses often won't make it through winter, even if they are rated hardy.

Fall may be an end for the garden in some respects but it's also a time of renewal. Many perennials can be planted or transplanted safely at this time, the better to get a jump on spring.

**The labor of planting tulip bulbs in fall results in this spring field of dreams, with a backdrop of crabapple blossoms.**

Take care of them by making sure they always have sufficient water, even during winter. Unlike much of the country, we can have many warm, sunny winter days and, if snowfall has been scarce, these late-planted perennials can be vulnerable to desiccation. Fall is also an ideal time to plant trees and shrubs. The advantage is that, although the soil is still quite warm, the plants are going dormant and have few or no leaves to support as they work at establishing their roots. As with perennials, build an earthen dike around each one and keep a hose handy all winter to fill it if necessary.

Fall also means it's time to plant bulbs. My head is filled with the promise of spring as I ruin the knees of yet another pair of jeans. Most gardeners concentrate mainly on tulips and daffodils (on which I'll elaborate in the next section), but some of the most long-lived and rewarding bulbs are the smaller ones. Tiny, early snow crocus may pop up as early as January when planted near rocks or paving. The number of flowers seems to double each year, with a mature clump showing up to a dozen flowers in white, yellow, lavender, or blue, often with darker contrasting outer petals in purple or maroon. Similarly, petite snow iris (*Iris reticulata*) behaves in much the same way and the flowers are incredibly pretty in shades of blue, purple, and white with little patches of orange or gold. You need to prostrate yourself to get a good look and a whiff of their sweet fragrance. Coming a bit later are the pendant bells of sky blue Siberian squill (*Scilla*), pale aqua-striped squill (*Puschkinia*), and pink or blue glory-of-the-snow (*Chionodoxa*). Grape hyacinths (*Muscari*) wait even a little longer to flower in late spring.

All of these small wonders exhibit good drought tolerance, bloom for decades, and seed themselves around in beds, borders, and even lawns. Don't be alarmed by this; it makes a boring green sheet quite lovely in spring. Many gardeners purposely make their lawns into a spring tapestry of bulbs. To do this, mow your lawn late in fall, pop the bulbs in by wriggling a dandelion digger or hori-hori back and forth in the grass to make a small hole, and water thoroughly. The bulbs coexist well with the turf. Just don't mow the lawn until the bulbs have ripened their foliage in May. It'll get a little scruffy, but hold off as long as you can and make sure you set the mower blade at the highest level to nip off as little foliage as possible.

Between planting bulbs and new shrubs and perennials and doing some rearranging and transplanting, a gardener should have his or her hands both full and dirty all fall. This is good because it will prevent you from getting in trouble. By trouble, I'm talking about hacking and whacking in some sort of seemingly autumnal rage. Sure, you can do a bit of clean up, pulling up frost-blackened marigolds and tomatoes. But perennials, grasses, and shrubs should be left alone rather than cutting them back, which may expose the crowns of the plants to bitter cold. Cutting back also encourages new growth, which is the opposite of what we want our plants to do in fall. Roses, for example, will respond to your pruning by sending out new shoots that are extremely vulnerable to cold. Often a cane will die back to the ground and often the entire rose will die. Save your strength for tucking bulbs in the ground before the snow flies. In late winter you'll be yearning to get back into the spring garden. Then you can get on with the whacking.

## THE GARDEN IN WINTER

As a gardener, I view winter as a season simply to be endured until I can get back to doing what I love. As a designer, I recognize both the value and possibilities of planting for winter interest. In the old days, when hacking the perennials to the ground was common practice, the only elements of visual interest in the garden were the bare silhouettes of trees and shrubs and the shapes of snowcapped evergreens. Now there's plenty to admire in a gardener's off-season. Ornamental grasses can be extraordinarily stunning in their sun-bleached, freeze-dried state. Many perennials and shrubs offer interesting architectural frameworks that are even more pronounced in winter when leaves and color have been stripped away. So many perennials feature beautiful pods and seedheads that are almost as beautiful as the flowers that preceded them. Yarrows, sedums, purple coneflowers, rudbeckias, globe thistles, and yuccas are among the best perennials that provide great winter presence. Some trees and shrubs get into the act as well, such as the bleached heads of 'Annabelle' hydrangeas, rose hips, orange firethorn berries, and hawthorn berries, as well as the rattling, burnished pods of golden rain tree and the dangling swords of catalpas and honey locust trees. The velvety red seed clusters of sumac are among my favorite winter sights. Yuccas and cactus also show especially well against a white winter canvas.

In winter, it always becomes apparent to me that I don't pay as much attention to evergreens as I should. I would never devote very much space to the largest junipers and pines—my small garden would soon be a very crowded place. But I certainly should add more dwarf conifers. Slow growing and never very big even at maturity, these fascinating and varied plants serve as anchors throughout the season. Their shapes and mass balance frothy flowers in summer and come into their own when the flowers fade. They can be especially impressive when juxtaposed with rocks and boulders, where their softness becomes most apparent.

Should we plan our gardens around their winter appearance? Of course not. Should we consider how our summer creation looks after the growing season? Absolutely. The "bones" of the garden become apparent. The shapes of trees and shrubs—and their placements—take on added importance. So do naturalistic features such as rocks, streams and ponds, formal pools, fountains, and pavings. Hedges, fences, arbors, trellises, and screens also loom large without the softening influence of vines and neighboring plants. Winter is the best time to scrutinize existing structures and plan to modify, move, or remove them to open up views or close off ones you don't wish to see next spring. For example, my neighbors across the street have created a view I choose to avoid. With screens and shrubs, I've managed to block this unfortunate view when spending time on my patio. Now my goal is to screen off my view of their carport, where they park their truck with personalized plates proclaiming their love for their favorite beer. A January day seems like an ideal time to contemplate how best to hide the brew.

It's also possible in winter to take a hard look at trees and shrubs that may need shaping or corrections. When they're cloaked with leaves, deciduous trees and shrubs are more difficult to analyze. I don't like guessing what the plant will look like if I remove a branch. I've often miscalculated where to prune when I can't see the tree for the leaves.

The best thing about winter is that it turns to spring. One of the most exciting moments of the year is poking around the garden on a sunny winter day, discovering emerging crocus and tulips and finding new growth on long-dormant perennials. Winter is finally on its way out—not without a fight, of course—and I take it as my cue to cut back the grasses and perennials to let the garden begin anew.

# ■ Vegetables and Herbs

Planting vegetables and herbs each spring makes me happy. You get so much from a packet of seeds. I don't grow it all from seeds because I'm crowded for space inside and those things that need a head start are more easily purchased as young plants. This includes parsley, peppers, eggplants, and tomatoes. It's best to draw up new planting schemes every winter so that, in essence, you "rotate" the crops. This helps to prevent the soil from becoming exhausted by the needs of one kind of plant and may help reduce pests and disease. Corn and tomatoes especially shouldn't be grown in the same spots for more than a few years in a row.

I like starting with a new plan each spring. I tackle the vegetable and herb plantings with the same enthusiasm as any other design. You can create pleasing patterns and combinations. Don't worry about putting vegetables in long rows as is customary. After all, you're not likely to harvest with a combine. You can also intermingle flowers for cutting or edible flowers such as nasturtiums, pansies, pot marigolds (*Calendula*), and dianthus. You must, of course, foreswear pesticides except for soap sprays. You will soon be able to create the most beautiful and tasty salads your guests have ever encountered. One of my favorites is a tossed salad of fresh green with violets, dianthus, and mandarin orange slices with honey mustard dressing.

## EDIBLES AT HIGH ELEVATIONS

Living in a ski town for several years did more than improve my form on the slopes. I learned about high-altitude gardening. Snow is a boon for attracting tourists—and for protecting plants. Snow makes an insulating blanket and helps insure the survival of many plants that might easily succumb to cold and wind without it. It keeps them at a constant temperature all winter—cold and dormant—rather than subjecting them to the alternating periods of freezing and thawing common to the plains and plateaus.

**Petals of pansies and red dianthus beautify both deck pots and salad bowls.**

Another thing I learned is that tomatoes were more difficult to grow than the most rare orchid on earth. My best success came when I grew them in big black plastic pots on my balcony where I could drag them in on cold nights and at the end of the season. Homegrown tomatoes are one of my culinary passions, but I rarely grew enough for more than a salad or two. But there are many vegetables and herbs that can enhance and expand the palate of gardening cooks at high elevations.

There's neither enough time nor heat in the mountains to succeed with warm-season vegetables and herbs such as corn, tomatoes, basil, squash, pumpkins, and peppers. But all the greens—lettuce, spinach, arugula, and mustard—grow beautifully, along with beets, carrots, runner beans, peas, dill, potatoes, and radishes. Many heat-loving herbs such as lavender, thyme, and oregano grow best if they're positioned near the shelter of rocks, stone walls, or foundations. A friend built an attractive stacked stone wall around her vegetable patch. The wall creates a heat trap that works with the intense high-altitude sun to grow excellent produce. Many of these edibles can also be grown well in pots—and you don't need to muscle them indoors every night.

## GETTING POTTED

Gardeners in the Rocky Mountain West sometimes feel a bit deprived because they can't grow plants they either used to grow somewhere else before they moved here or because they vacation in Phoenix or Florida. Exotic wonders aren't just for vacation snapshots. Container growing brings them right to your patio or balcony. Sometimes it takes a little time (and a few

**Far from home, lily-of-the-Nile blooms with abandon on a mountain valley patio.
The plant winters indoors in a sunny window.**

casualties) to figure out exactly what soil, sun, and fertilizer these outsider plants need. You have to decide where in your house they'll be housed for winter. It's all worth it.

It is perfectly natural and logical that gardeners go through phases. I know a former stockbroker who used to grow a few African violets and jade plants in his little home greenhouse. Then he discovered orchids. Now he owns the largest orchid nursery in our region. He found his true calling.

I'm somewhat more fickle. I've gone through more phases as a gardener than I did as a teenager. There's always something else with which to experiment. I'm all over the map, with succulents from subtropical deserts, Mexican dahlias, South African lily-of-the-Nile (*Agapanthus*), Mediterranean lavender, and Australian straw flowers. My current favorite is angel trumpets (*Brugmansia*), small tropical trees from South America with huge pendant exquisitely perfumed trumpet flowers. It took me awhile to know how best to grow them (you'll get my advice in the next section), but they thrill me to pieces. Surely you'll find plants and flowers that do the same for you.

There are several approaches to container gardening you may wish to consider. Boxes work well to dress up windows and deck railings. Hanging baskets dangle flowers and vines in the air. Single pots can serve as focal points at the end of walks or in front of or below garden architecture such as trellises and arbors. When it comes to groupings, you can either create combinations within each pot, or group solitary specimens to make a composition. Pot size, shape, and color can be utilized to further embellish your design. The great thing about pots is their porta-bility (well, at least you can drag them around with a little effort). A couple of times each summer I get the urge to tear everything up and put it all back together. I'm nuts, but I love it.

The key to success is to buy pots large enough to accommodate whatever you wish to grow. Big pots dry out more slowly, an important consideration in our dry, thin air and hot sun. Glazed pots are especially relevant for our region for this very reason, since water can't evapo-rate through the pot walls, only through the top of the soil. Glazed pots also offer an amazing array of design choices to complement any style of garden. They last for decades if you take care of them properly, and they'll keep rolling in if you hint properly before your birthdays and anniversaries and Christmas.

# ■ Water Plants in the West

The intensity of the sun, combined with a thinner atmosphere to penetrate, creates an almost ideal environment in the Rocky Mountain West for aquatic plants.

Some lucky people have natural streams and ponds on their properties. The rest of us have to start from scratch, digging, channeling water, and placing rocks strategically in an attempt to match nature's design. This is tricky. It's probably best not to just grab a shovel one morning and go dig a pond. Plan extensively and consult experts. I know an enthusiastic man who did neither and built a waterfall rivaling Niagara Falls. It dominates his backyard and makes so much noise that you need to shout to carry on a conversation. And the water crashes into the pond with such force that it pummels the water plants. You might want to take a more subtle approach. Or as I've suggested earlier, if your site doesn't lend itself to a naturalistic water feature, build a formal pond. Even if your gardening is limited to a patio or balcony you can still enjoy water gardening in big pots or little pools.

Whichever approach you take, you'll create distinct habitats for water plants. In a naturalistic setting, there are three habitats: the water's surface for floating plants, the pond's bottom for water lilies and lotus, and the water's edge for plants such as cattails that grow naturally just below and just above water level. In a formal pond you don't have a bank with mucky soil into which plants can thrust their roots, but you can still grow plants in pots that you cleverly stage on cement blocks or bricks at the correct level for them. (You can't just sink a pot of cattails 3' deep in the pond and hope for the best.)

Floating plants dangle their roots in the water and migrate around with the breeze. Water hyacinth, water lettuce, and duckweed are the most popular floaters. Water hyacinths have escaped into natural waterways in parts of the South and have become a nuisance; but there are no worries here, as these plants can't survive frost.

The star attractions of most ponds and pools are water lilies and lotus. Hardy water lilies, usually white or pale pink, grow naturally in many parts of our region. Tropical water lilies often display maroon stripes and streaks on their leaves that enhance a bright floral palette including pink, reddish violet, purple and yellow. Tropical lilies take more care; most need to be lifted and stored in a dark, cool, moist place in winter. So do lotus, which send their blue-green leaves and stunning pink blossoms above the water's surface (unlike the floating foliage and flowers

**LEFT: Even a small water feature supports many aquatic plants such as rushes and water hyacinths**
**RIGHT: Japanese iris thrives in the moist margins of a pond or stream.**

of water lilies). Water heats up slowly at high elevations—even with intense sun—and prime time for these flowers is August.

Edgy plants for your pond's margins include cattails, Japanese iris, yellow flag iris (*Iris pseudacorus*), and various rushes and reeds. These hardy plants contrast effectively with floating plants. The spiky leaves of Japanese iris grow about 3' tall and in early summer glow with exquisite flowers, showing a millennium of breeding, mainly in purple, lavender, and white. Muck-loving ligularias offer large, decorative bronze or green leaves and yellow or gold flowers on stems up to 4' high. Offering yet more contrast are tropical plants with big leaves, some with flowers equally bold, such as purple-flowering pickerel, elephant ears, and water cannas with an array of green, bronze, or variegated foliage and many flower colors. Most any canna can be grown successfully at water's edge.

Fish and plants go hand in hand (or maybe fin and leaf). When you start a new pond, go over to a friend's house with an established, healthy pond and scoop out a bucket of water. It will be full of the "good" bacteria that your pond needs. (If you bake sourdough bread you'll grasp this concept.) Ponds with fish and plants are never as crystal clear as a swimming pool. It takes weeks for a pond to establish its balance. Have patience.  The main trials and tribulations you'll face in your water world—besides algae—include, hail, raccoons, herons, and other varmints. It's a never-ending adventure.

# ■ Plants for Success

## PERENNIALS

### BLUE FLAX
*Linum perenne*
**Category: sun**
**Use: xeriscaping, borders, slopes**
**Soil: adaptable, somewhat dry**
**Hardiness: zones 3 to 7**
**Mature size: 14" tall by 12" wide**

A friend told me the story of a woman who asked to paint his garden. She started one morning filled with Monet-like passion. He glanced out the window in late morning and saw her frozen—brush in hand—looking back and forth from her canvas to the garden. His garden, dominated in that moment by blue flax, sunroses, and mullein, had gone missing on the painter.

---

**Blue flax (*Linum perenne*) with pink poppies and yellow yarrow.**

Those three plants had closed shop for the day. It's of no great concern unless you paint.

Blue flax grows wild in both Europe and North America, a simple pretty thing with sky blue flowers. The thin stems feature short, thin foliage more like spruce needles than leaves. You can sow seeds in fall or early spring or set out young potted plants from the nursery. (Save money; it's really easy to grow by just scattering the seed in the general area where you want some.) The flowers appear in late spring and bloom themselves out by midsummer. Take your pruners and cut the 14" stems back by half to produce another flush of bloom. You may wish to let the second set of flowers go to seed as this is a plant with good design instinct, sowing itself amongst other perennials and rocks where it looks best.

Sunroses and silver mullein (*Verbascum bombyciferum*) recommend themselves as companions (unless you expect a lot of afternoon guests), but blue flax invites all sorts of terrific combinations.

Potential problems: blue flax thrives on heat and drought, recovers quickly from hail, and is rarely if ever bothered by insects or disease.

## CATMINT
### *Nepeta x faassenii*
### Category: sun
### Use: borders, xeriscaping
### Soil: adaptable, somewhat moist to somewhat dry
### Hardiness: zones 4 to 9
### Mature size: 2' by 2'

Even nongardeners know about catnip, an herb that makes cats look silly. Few people know about catmints, plants of the same genus that make gardens look beautiful. The small, plain leaves are gray-green and refreshingly aromatic. Recent research has determined that their essential oils may be more effective than deet in repelling mosquitoes. There are no commercial applications as of yet. In the meantime I suppose it wouldn't hurt to plant some catmint near areas of outdoor activity or perhaps wear a sprig behind your ear as you garden.

I grow dozens of catmints throughout my borders. Starting in June, they create a lavender haze of small, mint-like flowers. They complement the stars of early summer such as shrub roses, daylilies, and yarrow, and promote a coolness that defies the thermometer. By August they look a bit tired, so the plants can be sheared back and fertilized to promote a new flush of bloom to usher in the fall season.

Two cultivars are quite similar; I can't tell them apart unless they're side by side. Both 'Walker's Low' and 'Six Hills Giant', despite the disparity in their names, can grow at least 2' by 2'. 'Blue Wonder' grows only 10" to 12" tall with sapphire flowers, making it a suitable candidate for the front of the border where it will seed freely. 'Walker's Low' and 'Six Hills Giant' seed only sparingly in my experience. They can be easily divided, however, in early spring just as they break dormancy. This is also the time to cut back old growth.

Potential problems: attractive to bees; perhaps this would result in odd-tasting honey.

'Six Hills Giant' catmint (*Nepeta* x 'Six Hills Giant') with chartreuse lady's mantle and pink *Stachys grandiflora*.

**ABOVE:** Dianthus (*Dianthus giganteus*)
**BELOW:** Giant sea kale (*Crambe cordifolia*) with snapdragons.

## DIANTHUS
### *Dianthus* spp.
**Category: sun**
**Use: borders, xeriscaping, rock gardens**
**Soil: adaptable, somewhat dry to dry**
**Hardiness: zones 3 to 7**
**Mature size: 8" to 12" tall by 10" to 16" wide**

Indispensable to Rocky Mountain gardeners, dianthus comes in many heights, shapes, and colors. There are many species and hybrids, sometimes loosely grouped together under the common name "pinks," but this is a bit confusing since many aren't even pink. Perhaps the most famous dianthus is the carnation, although the tall cutting types are pretty much bred for culture under glass and their heavy heads don't stand up under garden conditions. Fortunately, the distinctive spicy clove scent of the carnation is shared by its relatives, such as sweet William.

Mountain gardeners can grow sweet William (*D. barbatus*) to perfection. The colors range from jam red to magenta, rosy lavender, and other pink shades. Cottage pinks and cheddar pinks (*D. gratianopolitanus*) grow equally well on the plains or in the hills. With rounded mounds of dense silver-gray leaves (like those of blue spruce), their flowers practically smother the plants mainly in shades of pink, but some are white, salmon, or maroon. Some are two-toned with maroon centers on white petals or white spots on a rosy-red backdrop. All are tough, dependable, and water-thrifty.

Although the main flush of bloom comes early in the season, cut off the faded flowers and you'll likely get more. Leave a few seedheads for the plants to sow themselves. One of the most unusual members of this family, *D. giganteus*, grows almost 3' tall. It may seed sparingly, so move the volunteers into position to complement purple Rocky Mountain penstemon, lamb's ears, and catmint. Dianthus also looks spectacular with lavender, meadow sage, chartreuse lady's mantle (*Alchemilla vulgaris*), and roses.

Potential problems: neatness freaks will need to get out their sheers to cut back seed heads after the main flush of blooms.

## GIANT SEA KALE
### *Crambe cordifolia*
**Category: sun**
**Use: borders**
**Soil: adaptable, somewhat moist to somewhat dry**
**Hardiness: zones 4 to 7**
**Mature size: 5' by 5'**

Few plants can compete with giant sea kale for sheer dramatic effect. Its leaves might be mistaken for rhubarb except they're big—really big. Then come the sprays of small white flowers that appear a bit dainty in contrast to the enormous girth of the plant, somewhat like a tiara on a cow. The effect is marvelous when the flowers appear in late spring; they last for about a month. Finches love the subsequent feast of seeds.

Make sure you know where you want it when you plant giant sea kale. It puts down mighty deep roots that defy extradition, like a giant turnip. Seedlings should be pulled or relocated when first spotted as they may become inconvenient where they sow themselves, such as at the front of your border. This is definitely a back-of-the-border perennial, forming a great backdrop for any number of more petite companion plants. With those deep roots, giant sea kale can withstand periods of low rainfall. With its enormous mass, it serves as an excellent contrast in a dryland planting for all the fine-textured lavenders, artemisias, and ornamental grasses.

A dwarf by comparison, sea kale (*Crambe maritima*) is equally drought tolerant. Its main attraction is beautiful turquoise leaves with wavy edges topped by creamy white flowers in early summer. The leaves grow only 10" to 14" high, making it a delightful foil for sunroses, dianthus, creeping soapwort (*Saponaria ocymoides*), and other smaller dryland perennials.

Potential problems: moving a mature plant is problematical since they often go into shock. Remove almost all the foliage (which will wilt alarmingly anyway) and keep muddy moist for several weeks while the roots settle in. The plant may spring up again in the old spot from roots you couldn't excavate.

## HUMMINGBIRD TRUMPET
### *Zauschneria arizonica*
**Category: sun**
**Use: borders, xeriscaping**
**Soil: adaptable, somewhat dry to dry**
**Hardiness: zones 4 to 8**
**Mature size: 10" to 20" high with a spread of up to 2'**

Several different species of hummingbird trumpet range from Canada to Mexico. They bloom from north to south in fall in sequence with hummingbirds migrating south. They're all quite similar; your local nursery can supply the right one for the birds to visit the flowers in your garden. The tubular vivid orange blossoms make the most brilliant display in the autumn garden, a veritable beacon. The thin, narrow-leafed stems arch under the weight of the flowers, which nearly obscure the leaves.

The ultimate in xeric plants, hummingbird trumpets really thrive on heat and drought. Organically rich, moist soil doesn't suit them. They're comfortable planted between rocks, especially in cooler areas. Plant nursery-grown plants in spring so their roots can take advantage of the full season to get established. Late planting is pretty risky. And, like every perennial—no matter how xeric—they need steady moisture the first season while building their root systems. Needing only some grooming each spring, the plants are almost trouble-free. Picking partners for hummingbird trumpet is easy, with some blue mist spiraea for bright contrast and Indian blanket and yellow ice plant for harmony.

Potential problems: in some seasons, shiny black flea beetles may eat the leaves.

**Hummingbird trumpet (*Zauschneria arizonica*)**

ABOVE: Indian blanket (*Gaillardia aristata*) and California poppies.
BELOW: Lamb's ears (*Stachys byzantina*) with white feverfew, pink sweet William, and Indian blanket.

## INDIAN BLANKET
### Gaillardia aristata
### Category: sun
### Use: borders, xeriscaping, cutting
### Soil: adaptable, moist to dry
### Hardiness: zones 3 to 7
### Mature size: 16" to 20" tall by 12" to 20" wide

One of the most dazzling wildflowers, Indian blanket is native to the Great Plains. The flower petals of Indian blanket sport zigzag patterns reminiscent of Native American textile designs. (Sometimes you'll find this perennial called "blanket flower," which ignores the symbolism of the distinctive zigzags.) Drought tolerant and tough in all respects, it puts out a tireless stream of blooms throughout most of summer into fall. Suitable for cutting, the flowers are long-lasting in both the garden and a vase. Your help in deadheading will help to make sure it doesn't get caught up in seed production rather than flowering. Plants may self-sow if conditions suit them.

Most plants stay relatively compact with long, wiry stems to 16" to 20" tall. 'Goblin' is a shorter selection growing to just 12" or so, depending on conditions. Adaptable to clay or sandy soil and everything in between, Indian blanket seems at home when planted with other native plants such as blue fescue grass, scarlet bugler penstemon, and yucca. 'Burgundy' features wine-red petals without the characteristic zigzags, and 'Golden Sun' is its direct opposite, golden yellow without any red at all.

Potential problems: Indian blanket can get a bit gangly if overwatered and overfed; plants tend to flop over if the soil is too rich and water too plentiful.

## LAMB'S EARS
### Stachys byzantina
### Category: sun
### Use: borders, xeriscaping, edging, herb gardens, slopes
### Soil: adaptable, somewhat moist to dry
### Hardiness: zones 3 to 8
### Mature size: 16" tall by 2' to 3' wide

Seemingly more Muppet than plant, the silver "fur" of this charmer is irresistible to most of us. An old favorite in cottage gardens of the nineteenth century, this perennial nearly disappeared from cultivation when Victorians switched to more fashionable bedding annuals. It's back.

Lamb's ears' main attraction is its touchable silver leaves, although I'm fond of the upright stalks with small pink flowers peeking out from the stacks of what appear to be cotton balls. Some people don't care much for the flower stalks produced in late spring and early summer and choose to grow the nonflowering 'Silver Carpet', which stays about 6" high, or 'Countess Helene von Stein' with larger sage-green leaves (also called 'Big Ears', decidedly less class-conscious but a slap in the face to the German gardener who found it growing in her garden). It, too, is reluctant to flower.

Native to the Middle East, lamb's ears works well in herb gardens and rose gardens where it's often used for edging. I like it as a partner for most flowers since the silver leaves enhance their vibrancy. I cut back the flower stalks and dead leaves in late winter (it's like shearing sheep but not as strenuous) and they rejuvenate quickly. Plants slowly expand their territories; older ones may die out in the center. That's when they should be dug, divided, and replanted.

Potential problems: plants are both drought tolerant and lacking in pest and disease problems.

## LAVENDER
### *Lavandula angustifolia*
**Category: sun**
**Use: borders, herb and rose gardens**
**Soil: well-drained**
**Hardiness: zones 4 to 9**
**Mature size: 18" tall with about a 12" spread**

Everybody loves lavender, ever since an English soap maker named Yardley started adding the oil to his product in the eighteenth century. The English do indeed grow lots of lavender, but the perennial is native to the Mediterranean region. Obviously an adaptable plant (England and southern France have very different climates), lavender grows as well in our region if situated in warm, sunny, well-drained gardens; but plants only live about five years. The short, thin gray leaves—an adaptation to heat and sun—give a clue to its needs. Mountain gardeners often plant lavender near large rocks and foundations for extra heat.

Lavender has a woody structure like a shrub; drought tolerant, it grows best with even, moderate irrigation. The two most popular varieties for our region, dark purple-blue 'Hidcote', and lighter blue 'Munstead', are English cultivars. They're very pretty in formal gardens as a loose, low hedge or at the feet of roses. The pale pink shrub rose 'The Fairy' makes a perfect partner.

For drying, pick just as the flowers begin to open, bundle them, and hang them to dry. Place dried bundles in your linen closet or with sweaters. Lavender-perfumed sheets are the height of everyday luxury.

Potential problems: be careful when pruning as overdoing it can shock and kill the plants; they can rot out in winter if clay soil becomes waterlogged.

Lavender (*Lavandula angustifolia*) with thyme and 'Red Rubin' basil.

ABOVE: 'May Night' meadow sage (*Salvia nemorosa* 'May Night')
BELOW: Prickly poppy (*Argemone platycerus*)

## MEADOW SAGE
### *Salvia nemorosa*
**Category: sun**
**Use: borders, cutting**
**Soil: adaptable, somewhat moist to somewhat dry**
**Hardiness: zones 3 to 8**
**Mature size: about 30" by 30"**

A stalwart of the summer garden, meadow sage forms large blue or purple spikes of flowers. Showy all by itself, this perennial enhances every other flower in its vicinity. In late spring or early summer, each plant sends up many dozens of upright spikes covered with small flowers. They stay in bloom for up to six weeks, at which point you can cut them back by half, fertilize them, and let the show start all over again to carry the garden into fall.

Recent hot dry summers have tested the endurance of these European natives and found them exceedingly tough. The plants live for many years in a sunny, well-drained location but also tolerate a little bit of shade. Self-sown seedlings develop quickly and may even bloom the first year. Delightful with shrub roses, daylilies, dianthus, and lady's mantle, meadow sage is also beloved by honeybees.

'May Night' has the most intense coloration of the lot with deep purple-blue flowers. 'East Friesland' is a little smaller, and 'Blue Queen' is more the color of denim. 'Pink Queen' produces shell-pink blossoms. The flowers are suitable for cutting and are pretty with roses and daisies.

Potential problems: seemingly immune to pests and disease; they should be cut back in late winter to allow new growth to flourish.

## PRICKLY POPPY
### *Argemone platycerus*
**Category: sun**
**Use: borders, xeriscaping**
**Soil: adaptable, dry**
**Hardiness: zones 4 to 7**
**Mature size: 2' tall**

Some plants just weren't meant to grow in confinement. Such is the case with prickly poppy, a native beauty I've never seen in a nursery. Nature sowed the seeds in my garden and I couldn't be happier. By late spring the plant forms a silvery mound of gray and white foliage. The leaves and stems are indeed prickly and are topped by flowering stems to about 2' tall. Appearing mainly in June and July, the satiny white flowers measure about 2" across with a center of yellow stamens. The plants are short-lived but replace themselves with offspring, although young plants are difficult to transplant successfully. (Moisten the soil thoroughly and disturb the roots as little as possible.)

You'll sometimes see prickly poppies flowering along highway medians and railroad tracks, displaying a toughness that offers a clue to growing them. They don't need or want much supplemental moisture beyond what comes from the sky, and they grow best in what is often called "poor" soil, mineral-rich but devoid of organic matter. In other words, don't coddle your prickly poppies. At the end of the season, cut the seedpods and sprinkle the seeds where you want them in a sun-drenched spot. If nature hasn't sowed them for you, take note of where you see them growing in a vacant lot or near the off-ramp and pick a few pods when they ripen in early fall.

Prickly poppies consort equally well with other native wildflowers such as Mexican hat (*Ratibida columnifera*), Mexican evening primrose, and yucca as well as traditional perennials such as lamb's ears and meadow sage.

Potential problems: may rot if overwatered.

## PURPLE CONEFLOWER
### *Echinacea purpurea*
### Category: sun
### Use: borders, cutting
### Soil: adaptable, moist to somewhat dry
### Hardiness: zones 3 to 8
### Mature size: 2' to 3' tall by 1' to 2' wide

native to the Great Plains and a top performer in a wide variety of conditions, purple coneflower deserves top billing in nearly every garden. Many people take echinacea to benefit their immune systems; this species isn't harvested for that purpose. (*E. pallida* is the source for commercial echinacea and it can also be grown in the garden. The flowers are a paler pink and the plants slimmer and a bit taller.)

More pink than purple, the daisy-like flowers of purple coneflower feature a prominent center cone. It's ideal planted in large drifts in a border or meadow garden. Purple coneflower is long-lived and, where comfortable, will seed itself without becoming pesky. Don't bother to deadhead spent flowers as the plant will not rebloom reliably. The freeze-dried cones add decorative interest to both the fall and winter garden.

There are several named cultivars—the most distinctive is 'White Lustre', which grows a bit shorter than the norm, noted for its creamy white petals. The flowers of both pink and white forms make good long-lasting cut flowers. Blooming in mid- to late summer, purple coneflower makes a wonderful companion for daylilies, catmint, lavender, or Russian sage.

Potential problems: rarely bothered by pests or disease, this sun-loving perennial tolerates both wet feet and a degree of drought, although it will wilt and suffer during prolonged dry spells.

**Purple coneflowers (*Echinacea purpurea*) with goldenrod, mauve beebalm, and lavender hyssop.**

## PURPLE ICE PLANT
### *Delosperma cooperi*
**Category: sun**
**Use: rock gardens, xeriscaping, between paving stones, slopes**
**Soil: adaptable, moderately moist to dry**
**Hardiness: zones 5 to 8**
**Mature size: 8" by 18"**

Although ice plants are native to South Africa, they've certainly found a home in our region. First grown and introduced by Denver Botanic Gardens, ice plants have become garden staples in just a few short years. Small wonder. Well yes, they're both small and wonderful. Growing just inches tall, purple ice plant features plump succulent foliage with a crystalline iridescence like ice crystals, hence the name. Blooming through most of the summer, it boasts nearly fluorescent magenta-purple daisies. The foliage turns gray and plum in winter.

Growing wild in the mountainous regions of South Africa, purple ice plants demonstrate a greater hardiness than you might expect. Sun-loving ice plants grow well in almost every soil and don't require much water, fertilizer, or care. Creeping slowly along the ground, small plants may become as big as pizzas in several years.

Yellow ice plant (*D. nubigina*) blooms tirelessly in summer; its foliage grows tighter and more compact, turning red in winter. Both purple and yellow ice plant make excellent combinations with thyme, California poppies, and low-growing stonecrop, and can be underplanted with crocus or Siberian squills. New ice plant introductions include fuchsia 'Table Mountain', salmon-pink 'Mesa Verde', and 'Starburst', bright pink with a white center.

Potential problems: none.

## ROCKY MOUNTAIN COLUMBINE
### *Aquilegia caerulea*
**Category: sun**
**Use: borders, shade gardens**
**Soil: moist to somewhat moist, well-drained**
**Hardiness: zones 2 to 6**
**Mature size: 18" to 24" tall by 10" to 14" wide**

The star of western wildflowers, the Rocky Mountain columbine has probably sold as many postcards as the Eiffel Tower. Found in moist mountain meadows or at the edges of aspen groves, the columbine revels in cool temperatures, bright sun, and afternoon showers. High-elevation gardeners have no problem growing these lovely flowers with white petals and elegant sky-blue spurs that remind me of medieval jesters' caps.

The trouble with growing these beauties at lower, warmer elevations such as Denver, Grand Junction, or Salt Lake City is that they suffer when removed from their native habitat. Growing the plants in shade isn't much help as they yearn for sun and bloom only reluctantly. If you live in a warm area, don't despair. *A. chrysantha* 'Denver Gold' thrives in the dry heat, blooms

**ABOVE:** Purple ice plant (*Delosperma cooperi*) with blue fescue grass.
**BELOW:** Rocky Mountain columbine hybrids (*Aquilegia caerulea*)

Russian sage (*Perovskia atriplicifolia*) with black-eyed Susans and geraniums.

nonstop most of the summer, and can even stand some drought and light shade. As the name implies, the flowers are pale golden yellow but similar in all other respects to the blue-and-white mountaineer. 'Denver Gold' grows a bit taller as well, at 3' rather than 18" to 24".

There are a number of columbine hybrids such the 'McKana Giants' and 'Songbird' series that expand the color range to purple, lavender, red, pink, white, and yellow, most in combination such as yellow petals with red spurs. Rocky Mountain columbine and its hybrids are traditionally combined with other high altitude favorites such as sweet Williams, Shasta daisies, and painted daisies. 'Denver Gold' consorts beautifully with bellflowers, day lilies, and shrub roses.

Potential problems: aphids can curl the leaves and disfigure the flowers; leaf miners may also burrow inside the leaves, making irregular tracks on the foliage.

## RUSSIAN SAGE
### *Perovskia atriplicifolia*
### Category: sun
### Use: borders, xeriscaping
### Soil: adaptable, somewhat moist to dry
### Hardiness: zones 4 to 7
### Mature size: up to 5' tall by 2' to 3'

Russian sage made its debut in American gardens just a dozen years ago or so and quickly rose to prominence. No wonder—it's a superb perennial. Russian sage is not only long-lived and dependable, it possesses a refreshing aroma that is most noticeable on a warm breeze. Spouting a geyser of lavender-blue flowers from midsummer on, Russian sage deserves a spot in every garden. Small, gray-green leaves cover the bottom part of the stems and the tops form feathery sprays of small, woolly flowers. The sprays of flowers can be cut and used in arrangements but tend to drop little woolly bits on the table.

Russian sage seems to thrive best when put in baking hot spots such as up against a south-facing brick wall. But it's almost as vigorous under ordinary circumstances in a border, where it's lovely with rose mallow (*Lavatera thuringiaca*), daylilies, sunflowers, ornamental grasses, and purple coneflowers. After a few years, a plant may be as wide as a bushel basket. Russian sage needs only a late winter buzz cut, trimming the dead stalks down to the ground. You'd think that such an adaptable, vigorous perennial would sow itself liberally, but seedlings are rare. To make more plants, fork up an established clump and slice it into several pieces to replant.

Potential problems: nearly maintenance and pest-free, it can take everything nature throws at it, from clay to drought to hail.

ABOVE: Scarlet bugler (*Penstemon barbatus*) and catmint.
BELOW: Snow daisy (*Tanacetum niveum*) and 'Icicle' veronica.

## SCARLET BUGLER
### *Penstemon barbatus*
**Category: sun**
**Use: borders, xeriscaping, rock gardens**
**Soil: adaptable, somewhat moist to dry**
**Hardiness: zones 4 to 7**
**Mature size: 18" to 24" tall by 10" to 18" wide**

The pride of Rocky Mountain gardeners, penstemons grow here like nowhere else on earth. This is due, no doubt, to their native status. Gardeners outside our region covet them and envy us (perhaps the way we feel about their azaleas), but the penstemons really like our sunshine, low humidity, and mineral-rich soil.

Start with scarlet bugler (*P. barbatus*), an elegant flower with low, green basal foliage and long, arching spires of red tubular flowers much beloved by hummingbirds. Exceedingly drought tolerant, scarlet bugler blooms over an extended period if faded stems are removed periodically. Rocky Mountain penstemon (*P. strictus*) blooms in early summer with violet-blue bells above dark green basal leaves. Stunning shell-leaf penstemon (*P. grandiflora*) has tall 2' to 3' spikes of pink tubular flowers complemented by thick blue-gray foliage. All of these tall varieties of penstemon add height and color to the garden.

In the medium-height range—about 12" to 16"—are three lovely hybrids: salmon-pink 'Elfin Pink', rosy-red 'Red Rocks', and 'Pikes Peak Purple'. The latter two bloom with amazing vigor almost all season. On the shorter side, aptly named pine-leaf penstemon (*P. pinifolius*) puts on a vivid show of orange flowers on plants just 8" to 12" high. The selections 'Mersea Yellow' and 'Shades of Mango' are even prettier. Mat penstemon (*P. virens*) is just a few inches high with tiny gray-green leaves and small but profuse lavender-blue flowers in spring and early summer. These and other small species can be artfully combined with ice plant, blue fescue grass, and thyme along paths.

Potential problems: maintenance free, but can't handle wet feet or oppressive humidity.

## SNOW DAISY
### *Tanacetum niveum*
**Category: sun**
**Use: borders, xeriscaping, cutting**
**Soil: adaptable, well-drained, somewhat moist to somewhat dry**
**Hardiness: zones 4 to 7**
**Mature size: 20" by 20"**

Snow daisies are the backbone of my garden. I must have hundreds of them all over the place making domes of little white daisies from May to mid-July. Sometimes called silver tansies because of their attractive, finely cut gray-green foliage, the plants perform well under a wide range of conditions in sun and partial shade. Plants are generally short-lived, but never fear—

**'Wisley Pink' sunrose (*Helianthemum nummularium* 'Wisley Pink') and *Allium karataviense*.**

each one that succumbs is replaced by a hundred offspring. This would probably be annoying if I didn't like snow daisies so much.

After they fade, cut snow daisies back by about half and you'll likely receive another round of bloom for your trouble. Leave at least a few to set seed so you'll always have plants. Seedlings usually bloom in their second year. They're lovely in bloom—big drifts of white—and highly complementary to neighbors such as bearded iris, meadow sage, catmint, and shrub rose. You'd think such an easy-care perennial would have become widely popular, but it's not often found in nurseries. Call around or stop by my garden—I've always got plenty of seedlings.

Potential problems: pest- and disease-free; well-drained soil is preferable, as plants can rot out in wet clay, especially in winter.

## SUNROSE
### *Helianthemum nummularium*
### Category: sun perennial
### Use: borders, edging, rock gardens, slopes
### Soil: well-drained, somewhat moist to somewhat dry
### Hardiness: zones 4 to 8
### Mature size: 5" by 16"

I can't wait until the sunroses explode in late spring. The common name can be confusing. They don't look much like roses to me. They flower on spreading little shrubs bigger than a dinner plate but only a few inches tall. Pretty snuggled amongst rocks or at the front of a perennial border, they do like sun. Smothered in simple, five-petaled flowers for a month or more, the plants become radiant pools of red, orange, peach pink, yellow, or white each morning. By afternoon they fold their petals up for the day, so they're really best for early-bird gardeners.

Sunroses can be considered quite well-behaved; they rarely smother their companions, which might include thyme, sapphire blue Turkish speedwell (*Veronica liwanensis*), dragon's blood stonecrop, or hens and chicks. You might occasionally encounter seedlings. They're worth saving and relocating; the flower colors will be a surprise. There are several forms with double flowers that—to my mind—diminish the sublime simplicity of the originals. 'Wisley Pink' has salmon pink flowers above silvery leaves (most sunroses feature dark green leaves), 'Primrose Yellow' needs no explanation, and 'Saint Mary' is pristine white.

Potential problems: a really bitter winter can kill them. Where snow cover is unreliable, you may want to mulch them in late fall with a light material such as straw, pine needles, or shredded tree leaves. Remove mulch in spring with a rubber-tined rake just as the plants begin to leaf out.

## YARROW
### *Achillea millefolium*
### Category: sun
### Use: borders, xeriscaping, cutting
### Soil: adaptable, somewhat moist to somewhat dry
### Hardiness: zones 3 to 8
### Mature size: 18" to 24" tall by 16" to 36" wide

Yarrow is a perennial stalwart, performing tirelessly as long as it's planted in the sun. Native to many parts of the northern hemisphere, including the Rocky Mountains, wild yarrow is usually white or very pale pink. Low-growing, dark-green foliage makes dense, ever-expanding clumps. In early summer, myriad flat-top discs top stalks composed of many flowers. Lasting for up to several months, they're great for drying too. Pick them in their early prime, bundle them, and hang them upside down on a folding wooden clothes rack in a cool, dark place. Their dried flowerheads are very appealing in the winter garden as well.

I suppose yarrow could be criticized for being too aggressive, but that's not really fair. That only happens when it's pumped with too much water and fertilizer; then it starts to both spread and flop. You only have two chores: cut it back after the first bloom to get another, and trim back the plant in late winter in preparation for the summer show. Grow it lean and mean and it'll stay compact.

Modern selected varieties range from deep red and salmon pink to rose pink, lavender, pale yellow, and biscuit beige. Favorite cultivars include orange-red 'Paprika', salmon-pink 'Terra Cotta', and pale yellow 'Moonshine'. The 'Summer Pastels' mix encompasses all the colors of iced sherbets. The taller, golden-flowered yarrows such as 'Gold Plate' and 'Coronation Gold' are derived from the species *A. filipendulina*. These look great in combination with red-hot pokers (*Kniphofia*), ornamental grasses, and gay feather. Other good companions include snow daisy, shrub roses, silver mullein, and lavender.

Potential problems: yarrow is almost completely unaffected by drought, pests, disease, and weather. It can even recover from severe hail.

**Yarrow (*Achillea millefolium*) and blue spruce.**

# ANNUALS

✿

## ANGEL TRUMPET
### *Brugmansia* spp.
### Category: sun
### Use: patio containers
### Soil: potting soil, moist
### Hardiness: tropical
### Mature size: 5' to 8' tall by 2' to 5' wide

Angel trumpet, a small tropical tree grown as a potted specimen, is stunningly beautiful with 6" ivory, peach, or golden yellow trumpet-shaped flowers that possess an intoxicating fragrance something like a cross between roses and lemons. They're especially potent at night, when you might imagine yourself transported to a tropical destination. Break out the mai-tais. The flowers of *B.* x *candida* open ivory white, and over several days take on a delicate pinky-beige blush. 'Grand Marnier' opens lemon yellow, gradually changing to a peachy-gold. Flowers last just a few days but come in waves.

Before you leap and buy this plant, know that it has the appetite of a teenage boy, can't stand to dry out, and grows several feet tall. One mature plant rewarded me with one flush of more than 50 flowers in one week in August. I'm not kidding about feeding; for spectacular results, feed with a blossom-booster liquid formula weekly. Despite its tropical origin, angel trumpet doesn't need heat to perform well. If anything, it seems to thrive with cooler days around 70 degrees.

Angel trumpet does need a suitable sunny location indoors for winter, where it will continue to perfume your home, making air fresheners a thing of the past. Plant an angel trumpet in a big pot with a circumference of at least 20" initially. You'll need to bump that up every few years until lugging it in and out becomes too difficult. My eight plants grow in plastic or fiberglass pots, but I still need a dolly to move them.

Potential problems: the large leaves tempt spider mites and white flies on the undersides. Spray with a soapy solution to dispatch them.

Angel trumpet (*Brugmansia* spp.), flowering maple, and fancy-leaf geranium.

## BACHELOR'S BUTTON, CORNFLOWER
### *Centaurea cyanis*
### Category: sun
### Use: borders, xeriscaping, cutting
### Soil: adaptable, somewhat moist to somewhat dry
### Hardiness: annual
### Mature size: 10" to 16" tall

Decidedly old-fashioned, bachelor's button conjures images of grandma's garden, ice cream socials, and the era when gentlemen wore boutonnières on days other than their weddings. A European wildflower, bachelor's button is as adaptable as a dandelion (although young plants may prove difficult to transplant), but without intentions of world domination. Many so-called "wildflower" seed mixes contain its seeds and, although not an American native, bachelor's button possesses an unpretentious wildflower charm.

Like most of the flowers I champion, bachelor's button needs sun and little else. Adaptable to most soils from sand to clay, it performs best without a lot of fertilizer and water, which can cause it to grow tall and floppy. Depending on conditions, the slender plants start to bloom in late spring or early summer. The earliest flowers come from seeds sown in fall that germinate in late winter. You can also sow seeds in early spring. The plants may bloom themselves out by August. If you cut them back judiciously and give them a thorough watering, they'll usually repeat their blooming and last into autumn. Let this second batch of flowers go to seed for the next season. Pull the dead plants in late winter. Thin seedlings 5" to 7" apart for best development.

The most common form of bachelor's button is bright, clear blue—a terrific complement to summer perennials such as pink mallow (*Malva alcea*), hollyhocks, and rose campion (*Lychnis coronaria*)—but mixes contain flowers in pale blue, pink, rose, white, and chocolate maroon. All make fine cut flowers.

Potential problems: plants sometimes attract aphids, which curl the leaves and disfigure the flowers.

## BEGONIA
### *Begonia* x *hybrida* 'Dragon Wing'
### Category: shade
### Use: containers, beds
### Soil: organically rich, moderately moist
### Hardiness: tropical
### Mature size: 18" by 24"

Tropical, exotic begonias may seem an odd choice for the Rocky Mountain region, but they have much to offer. Probably not the best choices for high elevation (since they like heat), begonias perform well in both partial shade and sun. You may spot the popular wax begonias in formal bedding schemes in public parks. Named for their thick, waxy leaves (which make them more drought tolerant than their tropical looks suggest), the foliage is either bright green or deep bronze.

ABOVE: Bachelor's buttons (*Centaurea cyanis*) and Shirley poppies.
BELOW: 'Dragon Wing' begonia (*Begonia* x *hybrida* 'Dragon Wing')

**California poppy (*Eschscholzia californica*)**

The small flowers may be pink, white, or crimson. Tuberous begonias are the showiest types with flowers the size of cupcakes, ruffled and crinkled as if made of bright tissue paper.

A bit tricky to position, begonias grow best in pots in filtered sun; beneath a lacy honey locust tree is ideal. The begonia that really takes the guesswork out of growing them is 'Dragon Wing', a tough, gorgeous thing that takes sun or shade. Glossy green wing-shaped leaves grow on thick sturdy stems supporting many bright red flowers. My first plant is now three years old and just keeps growing and flowering with little attention from me. It blooms 365 days a year—wintering on my sun porch—but really revs up in the summer heat.

Because it's waxy and drought tolerant, this begonia works well in hanging baskets with sweet potato vine and trailing verbena. Easy to propagate from cuttings, 'Dragon Wing' now inhabits many of my patio pots in combination with variegated Cuban oregano, New Zealand flax, variegated ivy, and other tropicals that can be brought in for the winter.

Potential problems: may be nipped by frost if put outside too early or brought in too late.

## CALIFORNIA POPPY
### *Eschscholzia californica*
### Category: sun
### Use: xeriscaping, borders, slopes
### Soil: adaptable but on the dry side
### Hardiness: annual
### Mature size: to about 8" by 12" wide

How amazing the hills of southern California must have appeared, bathed in the golden glow of poppies, to the first Spanish explorers. Freeways and houses have dulled the effect somewhat, but we can all enjoy a golden moment in our own gardens. California poppy has always been one of my favorite flowers for both its elegance and simplicity. That it's easy to grow only increases my admiration.

Sparse, finely cut foliage features pretty flowers that can also appear in red, cream, and pink. Flowers spread their petals in the morning sun and close under clouds. The seedpods are long and thin and, when ripe, pop and shoot the seeds out. The seedlings are easy to spot and sometimes need to be thinned or they'll crowd each other out. A packet of seed is a great investment; you'll only need to buy one. The very best time to sow seeds is when the plants do it themselves—in fall. The seeds will germinate in late winter and start blooming a month earlier than those sown in spring.

California poppies are best left to their own devices. Sun is required, of course, but soil type doesn't matter much. If overwatered, the plants will get big and floppy and look horrid by midsummer. But even if you make this mistake, you can give them a good whacking back, reduce the water, and they'll start blooming again. The flowers span the seasons—spring, summer, and fall—and therefore look great with a parade of passing flowers from iris to verbenas to asters.

Potential problems: thin seedlings that come up too thickly to about 6" apart.

ABOVE: 'Sonata White' cosmos (*Cosmos bipinnatus* 'Sonata White') with lamb's ears.
BELOW: Dahlia (*Dahlia* x *hybrida*)

## COSMOS
### *Cosmos bipinnatus*
### Category: sun
### Use: borders, cutting gardens
### Soil: adaptable, somewhat dry
### Hardiness: annual
### Mature size: 4' to 6' tall by 1' to 2' wide

Some of our finest and most popular annuals originated in Mexico. When cosmos were first discovered by explorers and sent back to Europe, they were heaped with attention and subsequently grew to great heights with lots of food and water. Few people could even see the flowers that bloomed at the top of the plants. Let this be a lesson to us all: cosmos thrive on neglect. And for your lack of trouble, you'll receive a wealth of beautiful flowers in the garden and vases.

I have a penchant for simple, "unimproved" flowers. You can't improve much on the common cosmos, in the classic shades of hot pink, rose, shell-pink, and white. Sun loving and drought tolerant, cosmos adapt to most sites easily, even cooler conditions in the mountains. Seeds are the best way to go. Scatter in the fall or spring, or you can be a bit more deliberate if you'd prefer a row in the cutting garden. Plants usually grow from 4' to 6' in height, depending on your degree of neglect, and bloom unabated from midsummer to frost. You may wish to remove spent flowers to keep the plants at peak production. Cosmos self-sow with abandon; thin to about 12" apart to avoid overcrowding.

Cosmos are effective as backdrop plants for shorter annuals, perennials, and shrubs. The 'Sonata' series makes cosmos possible for small gardens since they grow just 18" to 24" tall with the same full-size flowers. These can also be grown in pots.

Potential problems: sticky wet clay soil is far from ideal; put in well-drained areas.

## DAHLIA
### *Dahlia* x *hybrida*
### Category: sun
### Use: borders, containers, cutting
### Soil: organically rich, moist
### Hardiness: tropical
### Mature size: 2' to 6' tall by 1' to 2' wide

Originally from Mexico (although their ancestors bear little resemblance to modern hybrids), dahlias like heat, humidity, and plenty of water. Not every garden can accommodate these requirements, so container growing is the answer. My garden doesn't receive enough moisture to support dahlias (nor is the soil organically enhanced), so I grow dahlias in big pots on the patio. The tallest types get too tall and gawky, but those bred to grow to 3' or less thrive.

I start the tubers indoors in black plastic pots in midspring. The trick is to fill the pot only halfway with soil, plant the tuber shallowly, and as it grows, add more soil to the top. In late

May, you have sturdy plants to go outside. When they're about 6" to 8" tall, pinch out the growing tips to encourage bushiness and branching. The tubers can be saved from year to year (in moist peat moss or wood shavings in a dark basement), so they make a good investment.

Compared to most plants in this gallery, dahlias need more food, water, and labor than the norm. They usually need stakes or some form of support because the stalks and flowers are heavy and easily subject to wind damage. This sounds like an inordinate amount of work (I'm nearly talking myself out of growing them next season), yet I'm quite taken with these buxom beauties, especially the vibrant red and orange-salmon ones.

Potential problems: earwigs get into the opening flower buds and shred them; leave a wet, loosely rolled newspaper at the base of the plant at night and the earwigs will hide in there for you to throw away in the morning.

## LARKSPUR
### *Consolida ambigua*
### Category: sun
### Use: borders, cutting
### Soil: adaptable, somewhat moist to somewhat dry
### Hardiness: annual
### Mature size: 3' to 4' tall by 8" to 14" wide

Gardens need spiky, upright plants as counterpoints to all the rounded and creeping ones. Many people rely on delphiniums for this purpose, but they have the drawbacks of being short-lived, needing staking, and requiring organically rich soil and moisture (mountain gardeners often grow superb delphiniums, so don't be put off by my words of caution). But not every gardener can meet these needs.

Larkspurs are closely related to delphiniums and perform many of the same duties without all the work. The inconspicuous feathery foliage becomes nearly obscured with long branching stems of spurred flowers. The standard cobalt blue larkspur remains one of the most lovely, intensely colored flowers in the garden. Many people prefer this color, but larkspurs also bloom in pink, rose, pale blue, and white. All make superb cut flowers.

Larkspurs transplant poorly, so you're probably best off to start with a packet of seeds. Broadcast the seeds in early spring; they germinate best in cool weather and can get by in partial shade. As with many annuals of this type, they will sow themselves in subsequent years and you'll count on them as a "perennial" annual. Larkspurs also perform beautifully in high-altitude gardens with plentiful moisture and look especially pretty with roses, red-hot pokers, snow daisies, lilies, and daylilies.

Potential problems: larkspurs can withstand heat, dry spells, and even hail.

**RIGHT: Royal blue larkspur (*Consolida ambigua*) with globe thistle and gold yarrow.**

ABOVE: Licorice plant (*Helichrysum petiolare*) with yarrow and gray santolina.
BELOW: Moss rose (*Portulaca grandiflora*)

## LICORICE PLANT
### *Helichrysum petiolare*
### Category: sun
### Use: containers, hanging baskets
### Soil: potting soil
### Hardiness: tropical
### Mature size: 4" by 2'

Some plants are like a good host: they mingle with everybody and make them look good. Licorice plants do that in container gardens. Their small, flat, rounded silver or pale green leaves, alternating along the trailing stems, enhance the color of any flowers planted with them as well as contrasting foliage such as bronze or bright chartreuse. Quick growers, licorice plants help give an established look to your patio by early summer, and also perform well in light shade. But they can be so vigorous when fed and watered consistently that they can overwhelm tamer companions. The common name is odd and misleading since they neither smell like or are a source for licorice.

Silvery licorice plants never steal the limelight and they let their companions shine. Interestingly enough, a cultivar with pale chartreuse leaves is named 'Limelight'. It's my favorite of the three, which also include a variegated form with both silver and chartreuse leaves, imaginatively called 'Variegated'. All are the best things to happen to hanging baskets since the invention of the hook. Bronze New Zealand flax (*Phormium tenax*) looks excitingly bold bursting through a froth of licorice plants, just as chartreuse or dark purple sweet potato vines contrast dramatically. Licorice plants are a natural to plant with canna lilies or dahlias, or to spill down the sides of pots and window boxes. They mix especially well with geraniums, verbenas, and the vigorous 'Wave' petunias.

Potential problems: may wilt without regular moisture.

## MOSS ROSE
### *Portulaca grandiflora*
### Category: sun
### Use: edging, xeriscaping, containers
### Soil: adaptable, somewhat moist to dry
### Hardiness: annual
### Mature size: 3" tall spreading to 6" to 10" wide

Moss roses aren't related to the true rose, nor are they fragrant. They creep along the ground, just inches high, with foliage that looks like plump spruce needles. The flowers do look a bit like single roses, about 1" across with satiny petals in lustrous colors. Moss roses can be purchased in single colors such as red, orange, magenta, pink, apricot, yellow, white, and even pink-and-white striped. I rarely buy annuals in mixed colors, but I make an exception for moss roses. Even if you do buy a single color, their offspring will likely flower in several different shades the next season. So why fight it?

The easiest way to grow moss roses is from inexpensive six-packs purchased after the threat of frost has passed. I usually feed moss roses at transplanting time to give them a little boost. Plant them along walks, between paving stones, or spilling from pots or hanging baskets. When they start blooming there's no stopping them, and they're a lovely addition to any sunny garden, consorting nicely with thyme, verbena, and stonecrop.

These humble annuals need heat to really shine. They're extremely adaptable as long as the soil is well drained and the site is sunny. Moss roses open as morning light hits them and close at sunset or when thick clouds shade them. The relatively new 'Sundial' hybrids are bred to ignore clouds and remain open. But the old-fashioned kind haven't lost their charm.

Potential problems: moss roses are heat, drought, and even hail tolerant, and I've never seen an insect (except bees) take the slightest interest in them.

## ORNAMENTAL KALE
### Brassica oleracea
### Category: sun
### Use: beds, borders, containers
### Soil: adaptable, evenly moist
### Hardiness: annual
### Mature size: 10" by 14"

Ornamental kale makes gorgeous heads of leaves—prettier than its edible kin—in fascinating colors with ripples, feathering, and streaks like nature's version of tie-dying. Each plant is slightly different and more interesting than the last. Some are deep burgundy red with pink or white markings. Others feature crinkled or frilled seafoam-green leaves with lavender or cream swirls. Others have broad, scalloped turquoise-blue foliage with pink and white veins emanating from the base of the plant.

If you've grown cabbage, you can grow kale. It can be grown from seed, either started inside early or in mid-May outdoors. You may wish to plant it originally in the vegetable garden, transplanting it in late summer or early fall to positions in the garden or pots. Consistent, even moisture ensures big, showy heads. Sunshine makes the colors glow.

Like most gardeners, I hate to see the end of the summer season. Putting together containers of ornamental kale helps me get over my depression. Just as heat-loving flowers fade, ornamental kale comes to the forefront. Impervious to the first frosts, it retains its beauty for a long season. Particularly valuable in pots, kale combines imaginatively with mums, pansies, and other cold-hardy plants to greet guests for autumn holidays. It can be also planted in beds among late-blooming asters, sedum 'Autumn Joy', and grasses. Depending on the severity of the winter and your remembering to water it, ornamental kale may last through the winter in the company of dwarf Alberta spruces.

Potential problems: caterpillars sometimes chew the leaves, but usually it's a minor problem; aphids may go after new growth.

**Ornamental kale (*Brassica oleracea*)**

**ABOVE:** Silver mullein (***Verbascum bombyciferum***)
**BELOW:** Sunflower (***Helianthus annuus***)

## SILVER MULLEIN
### Verbascum bombyciferum
**Category: sun**
**Use: borders, xeriscaping**
**Soil: adaptable, somewhat dry to dry**
**Hardiness: biennial, zones 4 to 7**
**Mature size: from 4' to 7' tall by 3' to 4'**

An unusual plant with a two-year life cycle, silver mullein produces a small rosette of gray leaves in its first season. In the second year, the rosette expands and sends up tall felt-clad stems studded with little primrose yellow flowers that open at dawn and close by noon. Seedlings are as silver as their parents—easy to spot and move around to create interesting compositions.

What do you do with such an unusual plant? It's not suitable for the back of the border because the low foliage wouldn't be seen and would perhaps get shaded out by taller shrubs and perennials. My solution is to plant it among low-growing annuals and perennials such as California poppies, blue fescue grass, ice plant, ponytail grass, and yarrow. Their fine textures provide excellent contrast to the imposing silver leaves. Silver mullein is extremely drought tolerant and thrives in dry, unimproved soil. You might try it in containers as long as you don't overwater it.

Another mullein is often found growing wild with a similar look but more sage-green leaves. *V. thapsus* was imported to mining towns in the West to grow for its flower stalks. They were cut, dipped in tallow, and used as torches in the gold and silver mines, hence the common name "miners' candles." The plants escaped into the wild and are considered a noxious weed. Silver mullein behaves much better than its cousin and has not been reported to make a break for our open fields.

Potential problems: insects don't want a mouthful of felt, so they avoid silver mullein. Its only nemesis is hail, which can puncture the leaves like a convertible top.

## SUNFLOWER
### Helianthus annuus
**Category: sun**
**Use: borders, summer hedges, edible seeds**
**Soil: adaptable**
**Hardiness: annual**
**Mature size: 4' or 5' tall by 1' to 3' wide**

Most of us take sunflowers for granted. They will, after all, grow with abandon along the highway or in a vacant lot. It's hardly a great achievement to grow sunflowers in your garden; they're just as likely to pop up by themselves. That's all the more reason to love them.

There isn't much to growing sunflowers. Sow seeds the first year in midspring; thereafter they'll do it for you. Pull unwanted seedlings in spring and plant from a seed packet if you want a particular variety instead of the hodgepodge you'll likely get. These heat-lovers have no special needs, but I'd suggest a moderate watering schedule and little or no fertilizer. The height of plants depends on conditions but most hit at least 4' or 5'. They'll stay the most compact with the least moisture, like the ones you see sprouting between cracks in the pavement. I grow a sunflower "hedge" around my corner lot garden. Friendly and colorful, it still affords me a little extra privacy.

It's difficult to improve on the lovely yellow annual, but it's been done. 'Italian White' is especially pretty with the dark center eye setting off its pale butter-yellow petals. 'Moulin Rouge' blooms deep brownish-red and commands attention, but for sheer drama try 'Mammoth Yellow'. Towering 10' to 15' tall, its flowers are as big as headlights and finches will hang upside down to peck at the seeds.

Potential problems: squirrels lust after the tasty seedheads.

## TALL VERBENA
### *Verbena patagonica*
### Category: sun
### Use: borders, containers, cutting
### Soil: adaptable, somewhat moist to somewhat dry
### Hardiness: zones 6 to 8
### Mature size: growing 3' to 5' high by 12" to 16" wide

Native to Argentina, this verbena grows in almost any soil and almost any sunny site as long as it doesn't get excessively dry. For those familiar with trailing verbena's flat, round heads of flowers, tall verbena is quite a departure. Little fluffs of lavender-purple flowers appear at the tops of pencil-thin stems growing several feet high. Plants take up very little space at ground level and won't shade out anything they tower above.

Tall verbena grows easily from seed. The ultimate in see-through plants, you can let it sow in any part of the garden—even near the front of the border or near a path—because it doesn't block the view. On the contrary, it just adds another layer of interest, a gauzy cloud if you like, to what you already have. I've read that some garden experts consider tall verbena a pest, but it's a matter of thinning and pulling unwanted seedlings in spring. Plants sometimes live over the winter and really put on a show the next year with a dozen interlocking stems.

Tall verbena makes a very good cut flower—especially when you need some height and airiness. I grow it in containers for that reason. *Verbena rigida* is a similar but much-reduced relative only 12" to 15" tall; common trailing types have been vastly improved for pots and hanging baskets as well as for weaving around the front of borders. They are available in lovely colors such as scarlet, hot pink, satin pink, and plum purple.

Potential problems: none; they even withstand hail.

Tall verbena (*Verbena patagonica*) with rice grass and silver mullein.

## ZINNIA
### Zinnia elegans
**Category: sun**
**Use: borders, containers, cutting**
**Soil: adaptable, moist to moderately moist**
**Hardiness: annual**
**Mature size: 10" to 20" tall by 8" to 10" wide**

Treasured for centuries, zinnias grow wild in Mexico, although the originals don't have the dozens of thickly packed petals like the modern hybrids. The colors remain mesmerizing and range from vibrant red, orange, violet, and lemon to pastel pink, salmon, and white to striped forms with white and yellow flecks on orange and red petals. Others bloom with tangerine-orange or golden flowers. There's even a celery green variety called 'Envy' that's quite extraordinary in arrangements.

Zinnias grow easily from seeds or six-pack transplants in a sunny spot. There's no hurry in getting them planted in the spring as they need heat to thrive and will stunt if set out or transplanted when night temperatures and soil are too cool. Zinnias do best with consistent, even moisture and are easily integrated into cutting or vegetable gardens as a constant source of bouquets.

A new class of zinnias has come into play in the past several decades derived from another wild Mexican species, *Z. angustifolia*. Rather than growing on tall upright stems like the cutting varieties, these zinnias spread to make a 10" by 10" mound. 'White Star' is a popular cultivar featuring single creamy-white flowers with golden eyes. They can be used in both beds and containers but aren't especially good for cutting as the stems are quite short. By crossing these two kinds of zinnias, breeders have created the 'Pinwheel' series, which stay low but incorporate the more brilliant colors of the cutting zinnias.

Potential problems: *Z. angustifolia* types are basically immune to mildew but the cutting types are still somewhat susceptible. Chewing insects—grasshoppers and caterpillars—are an occasional nuisance.

**Zinnia (*Zinnia elegans*) with burgundy fountain grass.**

'Rosemond Cole' canna lily (*Canna* x *generalis* 'Rosemond Cole') with marigolds, eucalyptus, and artichoke.

# BULBS

## CANNA LILY
### Canna x generalis
**Category: sun**
**Use: beds, containers**
**Soil: organically rich, moist**
**Hardiness: zones 6 to 10**
**Mature size: 3' to 6' by 1' to 2'**

Gardeners in cold winter climates can grow canna lilies as annuals, but they really aren't true annuals like petunias or marigolds. Cannas are bulbous perennials that grow from rhizomes. Customarily planted after the danger of frost has passed in late spring, they grow by leaps and bounds as the thermometer climbs. If you water sparingly in your garden, you'll probably grow cannas best in large containers on a sunny patio where you can lavish them with food and water. Cannas serve as excellent backdrops for other potted patio plants such as flowering maples, salvias, and begonias.

I recommend starting the rhizomes indoors in gallon pots filled with rich potting soil about a month before the last average frost. Then in autumn, let the foliage go through the first freeze, trim off the foliage, and store the rhizomes over the winter in moist wood shavings or peat moss in a dark cool place such as a basement. Wet them down every few weeks to keep them from withering. Cut the rhizomes in pieces so that each has several growing "eyes" before you replant each spring. (Surprisingly, cannas planted in the ground near west or south foundations usually survive the winters and grow stronger and thicker each year.)

Foliage is the thing when it comes to cannas. Some have dramatic, bronze-toned leaves such as 'Wyoming', growing to 6' tall with orange flowers. Much smaller bronze-leaf cannas include 'Futurity Rose' and 'Futurity Pink', growing just to 2' tall. Equally dramatic are the variegated-leaf cannas such as 'Pretoria', with orange flowers atop yellow-and-green striped leaves, and 'Tropicanna', with bronze-and-salmon foliage and orange flowers.

Potential problems: insects rarely bother cannas; the worst fate that can befall them is hail.

**ABOVE: 'Carlton' daffodil (*Narcissus* 'Carlton')**
**BELOW: Gayfeather (*Liatris spicata*)**

## DAFFODIL
### Narcissus spp.
### Category: sun or shade
### Use: borders, cutting, naturalizing
### Soil: adaptable, somewhat moist to somewhat dry
### Hardiness: zones 3 to 8
### Mature size: 8" to 12" by 6"

Daffodils are the quintessential spring flower and, in our region, an excellent choice. It seems odd that such beloved flowers would be poisonous, although I've never heard of pets or children eating them. Visit your garden center in fall to purchase bulbs and allow more time that you think you'll need, because you'll be racked with indecision over the dozens of daffodil possibilities.

Daffodils perform well in almost any soil, in sun, or beneath deciduous trees before they leaf out for summer. Unlike tulips, however, which like a dry, hot summer baking, daffodils prefer a milder, moister summer even when they're dormant. For this reason avoid areas that dry out completely in summer. Daffodils are ideal for planting in meadow gardens, in rough grass around fruit trees, or near a stream or pond. Resist the urge to cut or pull their foliage until it has gone brown and withered, indicating that the bulb has renewed itself for the next spring.

'Carlton' and 'King Alfred' represent the classic yellow daffodil, and 'Ice Follies' is a white variety with an equally strong constitution. 'February Gold' is indeed a treasure but gleams a bit later in spring than its name implies. 'Actea' has white petals with a short, orange-ringed cup. In borders, overplant daffodils with creeping phlox, Turkish speedwell, and other low-growing perennials that flatter them.

Potential problems: unlike tulips, daffodils are usually left alone by deer and rodents due to their poisonous nature.

## GAYFEATHER
### Liatris spicata
### Category: sun
### Use: borders, cutting
### Soil: adaptable, somewhat moist to somewhat dry
### Hardiness: zones 3 to 8
### Mature size: up to 3'

Plant one walnut-sized bulb this year and in about three years you'll be amazed by a thick clump with eight to a dozen imposing purple plumes of gayfeather. Native to the southeastern states and found mostly in meadows, gayfeather grows bolt upright, each stalk covered halfway up with thin green leaves. Buds take over midway and, contrary to almost every other plant, open from the top down rather than the reverse. Individual flowers are composed of fine purple filaments that impart a feathery appearance in mid to late summer.

Gayfeather is somewhat drought tolerant but thrives with a consistent moisture supply. Our native gayfeather, *L. punctata*, does revel in heat and drought. Diminutive in all aspects—just 12" tall—compared to its showier cousin, it's still very pretty and effective in dryland plantings with Indian blanket and native grasses. Leave the dried tan flower stalks to punctuate the fall and winter landscape but cut back dead stalks in early spring.

Extremely long lasting, gayfeather has become a florist's favorite in arrangements. In the garden, it's a welcome counterpart to rounded and creeping plants such as nasturtium, thyme, and catmint. The glowing violet-purple color pairs impressively with orange and yellow flowers such as black-eyed Susans, daylilies, golden yarrow, red-hot poker, and Mexican sunflower. A white form called 'Floristan White' makes a pretty picture with lilies, lavender, pink 'Clara Curtis' daisies, and lamb's ears.

Potential problems: few or no concerns about insects or diseases.

## GRAPE HYACINTH
### *Muscari botryoides*
**Category: sun or shade**
**Use: borders, cutting, shade gardens**
**Soil: adaptable, moist to dry**
**Hardiness: zones 3 to 8**
**Mature size: 8" by 3"**

If you own a crabapple tree or are considering planting one, plant grape hyacinths beneath it. They bloom simultaneously in spring, the falling pink crabapple petals making a serendipitous combination with the spikes of blue flowers below, and they possess a unique, sweet musky fragrance. Native to eastern Europe and central Asia, grape hyacinths indeed resemble tiny grapes. The flowers are rounded bells in shades of blue and purple as well as white with a constricted opening at the bottom and a white-toothed rim, packed densely on leafless spikes rising from narrow basal leaves. Among the most charming of all flowers, they make cute little bouquets on the nightstand or vanity.

Several species of grape hyacinths can be purchased and planted in fall, when, oddly, their foliage appears. This trait is put to use by clever gardeners to outline where they've planted tulips and daffodils. That way they won't impale these bulbs as they plant new bulbs or rearrange perennials in fall. Extremely adaptable, the bulbs can be planted in sun or light shade. The grape hyacinths will quickly form large clumps and sow new plants. The foliage fades unobtrusively and once, planted, grape hyacinths require no maintenance. Extremely durable and long-lived, they thrive, seed themselves, and persist for generations.

If you follow my crabapple suggestion, you can further enhance the picture by planting dead-nettle, hostas, lungwort, vinca, and other shade perennials in a tapestry of complementary foliage and flowers.

Potential problems: seemingly immune to insects and disease.

Grape hyacinths (*Muscari botryoides*) with foliage of lady's mantle and colchicum.

ABOVE: Iris (*Iris pallida*) with ice plant and scarlet bugler.
BELOW: Star of Persia (*Allium christophii*) with smoke bush

## IRIS
### *Iris pallida*
**Category: sun**
**Use: borders, slopes, cutting**
**Soil: adaptable, somewhat moist to somewhat dry**
**Hardiness: zones 3 to 7**
**Mature size: 8" to 2' by 10" to 16"**

Gardeners have been growing and loving iris for many centuries. The hybrids we grow today are of somewhat mysterious origin from species native to central Europe and the Middle East. They're tough. Early settlers to the Rocky Mountain region brought the rhizomes with them on covered wagons and planted them around their homesteads. Even today you can occasionally spot a crumbling house on the prairie with iris and lilacs still flowering each spring.

Iris lovers sometimes get carried away and end up with 300 varieties of their fave and not much else. Try to control yourselves. Plant them in a sunny location—they're not too fussy about soil—and leave them alone for three or four years except to trim off the flowering stalk after the flowers fade. Never cut the foliage in a fan shape unless you're dividing and transplanting (after they finish blooming is the best time), which they'll need every three to five years.

Some people aren't too crazy about iris foliage, but the variegated forms of purple-flowering *Iris pallida*, striped with white or yellow on the spears, make them a valuable addition throughout the growing season, and they work well with creeping phlox or creeping speedwell. Because its bloom time is in late spring and early summer, iris takes the stage with snow daisies, dianthus, shrub roses, and peonies. They offer an encore performance in fall, making them hallmarks of two seasons. Don't forget about the dwarf and intermediate varieties that can extend the iris season by several weeks.

Potential problems: borers sometimes plague iris growers in other parts of the country, but rarely in our region.

## STAR OF PERSIA
### *Allium christophii*
**Category: sun to partial shade**
**Use: borders, drying**
**Soil: adaptable, moderate to moist**
**Hardiness: zones 5 to 8**
**Mature size: 8" to 10" tall**

Native to the Middle East, in late spring this ornamental onion produces round flowerheads the size of grapefruits or larger, composed of hundreds of starry metallic lavender flowers. There's no onion odor to worry about (as with other ornamental onions) unless the stems or leaves are picked or bruised. In the fall, plant star of Persia bulbs about 5" deep and close to the front of the border or near walks so you can best appreciate them. Some people remove the flower-

**Tulips (*Tulipa vvedenskyi*) with purple rock cress.**

heads after the flowers fade, but I leave them for awhile; they eventually break off, roll around, and spread their seeds.

Perhaps the best known allium—and tallest—is *A. giganteum*. It's the purple puffball on a 4' stem so often found on the cover of bulb catalogs. *A. aflatunense* is smaller and shorter at 24" to 30" high. 'Purple Sensation' has tennis ball–sized bright violet heads. 'Globemaster' blooms with a purple flowerhead nearly the size of a cantaloupe on 16" to 24" stems. All of these lollipop alliums can be scattered in groups of five or so throughout the garden for a whimsical effect, "floating" above clumps of perennials and grasses.

Potential problems: maintenance free and very deer and mice resistant, as critters don't like the onion flavor.

## TULIP
### *Tulipa* spp.
### Category: sun
### Use: borders, xeriscaping, cutting
### Soil: adaptable, somewhat moist to dry
### Hardiness: zones 3 to 7
### Mature size: 6" to 16" by 6"

Surprisingly, tulips are not native to Holland. They grow wild in central Asia, largely on grassy high plains and plateaus with clay soil, cold winters, and hot, dry summers that bear a striking similarity to our own. The trick to growing great tulips is to select the ones that retain the survival skills of the wild tulips of central Asia.

Tulips don't need as deep planting as usually recommended; 4" to 5" deep is just fine for the hybrids (or about 2" or 3" for the species). I prefer to scatter a dozen or so at a time (for an unstudied, natural look) and then pop them into the soil with a dandelion digger or Japanese fisherman's knife. You can also dig a hole big enough for five or six bulbs spaced 4" apart for a thick, bouquet-like clump. Bulbs emerge beautifully through ground covers like basket-of-gold, creeping phlox, stonecrop, sweet woodruff, thyme, creeping or Turkish speedwell, or vinca.

Wild tulips have much smaller bulbs that are easier to plant. They include apricot-colored *Tulipa batalinii*, starry yellow and white *T. tarda*, and candy-striped red *T. clusiana*. Other smaller, tough red tulips hybrids are 'Red Riding Hood', 'Shakespeare', and 'Waterlily'. If you want the classic tall, bright Holland tulips, the best are the Darwin hybrids such as Corvette red 'Apledoorn' and shiny yellow 'Golden Apledoorn'. Also recommended are the appropriately named lipstick pink 'Elizabeth Arden', rosy red 'Big Chief', 'Pink Impression', 'Salmon Impression', 'Orange Sun', and yellow 'President Kennedy'.

Potential problems: tulips are the most vulnerable of the bulbs to wildlife. Squirrels, mice, voles, and deer relish them.

# GROUND COVERS

✍

## BLUE OAT GRASS
### *Helictotrichon sempervirens*
### Category: perennial
### Use: borders, cutting
### Soil: adaptable, somewhat moist to somewhat dry
### Hardiness: zones 3 to 7
### Mature size: 12" to 15" tall (seedheads rise to 3')

Ornamental grasses make up a high proportion of our native vegetation. Blue oat grass has much to recommend it: its moderate size, steely blue blades, and ability to associate gracefully with perennials without overwhelming them.

Blue fescue grass (*Festuca glauca*) grows half as tall with very thin, powder blue blades. It's extremely drought tolerant, and its diminutive stature calls for it to be planted in casual drifts near pathways. Ponytail grass (*Stipa tenuissima*) possesses an even finer texture and is sometimes called Mexican hair grass. Bright chartreuse green, ponytail grass bleaches to blond in winter. Maiden grass (*Miscanthus*) isn't as water thrifty as most grasses but forms clumps 4' to 8' tall pretty white or yellow-striped foliage. Burgundy fountain grass (*Pennisetum setaceum* 'Rubrum') is not as hardy in our region, but is such a stellar performer that it's worth adding to beds, borders, and especially containers where its reddish-brown foliage and feathery plumes accent bright annual flowers such as zinnias and salvias. I admire blue oat grass and blue fescue with dianthus, garden sage (*Salvia officinalis*), ice plant, thyme, and 'Autumn Joy' stonecrop.

The selection of grasses has expanded greatly at garden centers in the past decade. I've only touched on a few, but you'll likely find a few dozen. Make sure you're prepared for their ultimate sizes. Aside from their ease of care (just cut them down to the ground in late winter), the seedheads often add grace to both fresh and dried arrangements.

Potential problems: some varieties such as ponytail grass may seed aggressively where conditions are ideal.

**Blue oat grass (*Helictotrichon sempervirens*) with snow-in-summer.**

**ABOVE: Hen and chicks (*Sempervivum* spp.)**
**BELOW: Thyme (*Thymus* spp.), snow-in-summer, and dianthus.**

## HEN AND CHICKS
### *Sempervivum* spp.
### Category: sun
### Use: rock gardens, edging, xeriscaping
### Soil: very adaptable
### Hardiness: zones 3 to 8
### Mature size: 8" to 12" tall by 6" wide

The central rosette of hen and chicks is composed of thick, fleshy leaves arranged symmetrically. Small offshoots are clustered around the central plant, like chicks crowding around a mother hen. The small, star-shaped flowers are usually yellow, rose pink, or brick red. The common species, *S. montanum*, is dark green with reddish-brown on the edges and points of the leaves. The foliage of *S. tectorum* is completely maroon red. Other species and hybrids display smaller leaves and more compact structures. Called houseleeks in Europe, the common form is said to have plugged holes in thatch roofs.

Hen and chicks endeavors to live up to its scientific name *Sempervivum*, which means "live forever." They're so tough they'll grow on a sidewalk. Hen and chicks is also the superglue of the plant world. Once in place, they cement together on rock walls, between paving stones, or along paths. Perhaps you know someone who'll be happy to tease some chicks away from the mother plant, or you can buy them at your local nursery. Growers that specialize in rock garden plants will likely offer more selections. The bold rosettes contrast effectively with smaller plants used for the same purpose such as dragon's blood stonecrop, ice plant, mat daisy (*Anacyclis depressus*), and thyme. I plant them at the base of blue fescue grass; it's a perfect pairing.

Potential problems: the ultimate in easy-care plants; just cut off spent flower stems.

## THYME
### *Thymus* spp.
### Category: sun
### Use: Herb gardens, edging, xeriscaping, between paving stones
### Soil: well-drained, somewhat moist to dry
### Hardiness: zones 5 to 8
### Mature size: 2" to 12" by 10" to 16"

Gardeners don't like bare soil. It invites weeds to sprout and has an unfinished look. Many novice gardeners load up the car with bags of bark mulch that they spread to cover bare ground. Plant thyme instead. Native to the Mediterranean region, it's nature's idea of living mulch. It will bloom periodically with tiny but showy pink, lavender, or white flowers and look fresh long after the bark has faded and floated down the gutter. And, it has a refreshing aroma exploited by cooks.

Some forms of thyme creep on the soil surface while others grow like tiny shrubs 8" to 10" high. The lowest forms are suitable for growing between paving stones. Woody types may need a quick pruning job in spring. All revel in heat and periods of low rainfall. With the exception of woolly thyme (*T. pseudolanuginosis*), which takes partial shade and rarely blooms, they require full sun. Thyme is wonderful at the front of borders, growing amongst rocks, and making tapestries with other low growers such as dianthus, snow-in-summer, stonecrop, and hen and chicks. Among the showiest are lemon thyme (*T.* x *citriodorus* 'Aureus'), with tiny yellow variegated leaves and pale lavender flowers, and its white-variegated counterpart 'Silver Queen'. 'Pink Chintz' blooms profusely on plants just 2" to 3" tall. 'Elfin' thyme (*T. praecox*) is tiny in all respects, down to its little purple blossoms, and works well between flagstones.

Potential problems: a hard winter without snowcover may spell doom for some of the taller, woody varieties but, in general, the plants are hardy, long-lived, and carefree. Heavy clay soil holds too much moisture and may also present a problem for winter survival.

## WINE CUP
### *Callirhoe involucrata*
### Category: sun
### Use: xeriscaping, borders, slopes, retaining walls
### Soil: adaptable, somewhat dry
### Hardiness: zones 4 to 8
### Mature size: 6" tall

One of the prettiest of the western wildflowers, wine cup is finally enjoying the popularity it deserves. A sprawling perennial from the short grass prairies, it can grow several feet in every direction from its center, entwining other perennials in its embrace although not being too overwhelming. Settlers called it buffalo rose as it was often found in the moist soil near buffalo wallows, low spots where melting snow and summer rain collected and buffalo drank and took mud baths. The cup-shaped single flowers are about as big as a fifty-cent piece, vibrant wine pink with a white center. Heavily produced on rambling stems with dark green leaves from early summer to frost, they're especially impressive tumbling from a sun-drenched retaining wall or across big boulders. There's also a white-flowering form with shiny, satiny petals.

Like most wildflowers, wine cup thrives on benign neglect. Although it will survive a rainless summer, it performs best if given some extra water during periods of high heat and no rain. Plant nursery-grown stock in spring or early summer in any type of soil with room to roam. Clean up last year's dry stems in early spring as the plants break dormancy. Ideal companions include sunroses, blue flax, Indian blanket, ponytail grass, blue fescue grass, and shorter daylilies such as golden yellow 'Stella d' Oro'.

Potential problems: I've occasionally seen shiny black flea beetles bother the leaves, but their populations rise and fall in approximate five-year cycles and are generally not a problem.

Wine cup (*Callirhoe involucrata*) with clustered bellflower and daylilies.

# SHRUBS

## BLUE MIST SPIRAEA
### *Caryopteris* x *clandonensis*
**Category: sun**
**Use: borders, xeriscaping**
**Soil: adaptable, somewhat moist to dry**
**Hardiness: zones 4 to 8**
**Mature size: 3' to 4' by 3'**

Blue mist spiraea is a tough shrub for tough times. The foliage is oval, toothed, and dusty green, just right to enhance the explosion of small tubular flowers arranged in whorls all along the stems. Seedlings are often found in gardens with sandy soil but not so much in clay. Easy to transplant when young, they'll reach maturity in three to five years. Appearing in midsummer, the flowers bloom tirelessly well into fall. For best results, trim the woody stems back in late summer to about 10" in height. This promotes bushiness, and shrubs will quickly regrow into a 2' by 2' dome, perhaps doubling this in a great growing season.

There are several forms of this shrub—some deeper blue than others—but the standout is 'Worchester Gold'. Its golden chartreuse leaves add to the garden at the first part of the season but really set off the blue flowers when they appear. 'Worchester Gold' (pronounced woos-ter, like woos-ter-sheer sauce) is even better equipped to deal with periods of low rainfall than the ordinary green-leaf types. It would be stunning with the yellow and green variegated yucca or the similarly striped variegated iris (*Iris pallida* 'Variegata') as well as the variegated garden sage (*Salvia officinalis* 'Icterina'). Then I think I'd throw in some blue oat grass or blue fescue to contrast all that gold. This would make a water-thrifty grouping that would appear fresh and spring-like no matter the heat. Needless to say, blue mist spiraea also makes a perfect backdrop for summer perennials such as Indian blanket, purple coneflower, and penstemons.

Potential problems: will look scraggly unless cut back every spring.

## BUTTERFLY BUSH
### *Buddleia davidii*
**Category: sun**
**Use: borders**
**Soil: adaptable, somewhat moist to somewhat dry**
**Hardiness: zones 5 to 8**
**Mature size: 4' to 8' by 3' to 5'**

Everybody loves butterflies; this shrub will entice them into your garden. Looking very much like a lilac, butterfly bush differs by blooming from midsummer into fall. Most of these Chinese natives have green, lance-shaped leaves. The height of butterfly bushes varies from year to year.

ABOVE: Blue mist spiraea (*Caryopteris* x *clandonensis*) with sunflowers.
BELOW: Butterfly bush (*Buddleia davidii*) with white woodland tobacco and tall verbena.

After three or four mild winters with minimal winter die-back, the shrubs may reach 8' or 10'. After a harsh winter, when you may be forced to prune back the deadwood to just 12" or so, your shrub may hit only 3' or 4'.

Plant butterfly bush with enough room to spread out and mature. Spring planting is best, as the roots need time to develop and settle in before winter. When pruning in spring, wait to see how far up leaves develop on the branches. Cut at that level, evening out the branches to create a top-dome shape.

Colors range from white 'Peace' to rosy 'Pink Pearl' and violet-purple 'Black Knight'. Another marvelous species currently enjoying great popularity is fountain butterfly bush (*B. alternifolia*). Growing into an arching, spreading shrub up to 10' by 10', its graceful branches with attractive gray-green leaves hold rosy lavender flowers at the tips in early summer. This species is perhaps the toughest, most drought tolerant, and most durable of all the butterfly bushes. It also appears to exhibit a greater degree of drought tolerance. All butterfly bushes bloom profusely and look handsome with Helen's flower (*Helenium autumnale*), pink mallow (*Malva alcea*), and ornamental grasses.

Potential problems: late-planted shrubs may have trouble surviving winter.


# LILAC
### *Syringa vulgaris*
### Category: sun
### Use: hedges, borders, xeriscaping, cutting
### Soil: adaptable, somewhat wet to dry
### Hardiness: zones 3 to 7
### Mature size: up to 10' with a spread of 6' to 8'

It isn't spring without lilacs. Settlers first brought these shrubs to the Great Plains on wagon trains, with the cuttings stuck in potatoes to keep them alive. The cuttings took to the clay, alkaline soil (similar to that in the lilac's native central Asia) and have become part of our gardening heritage. The heart-shaped green leaves are almost leathery in texture, helping them to retain moisture. The panicles of flowers bloom in midspring, depending at what elevation you live. Long-lived and amazingly tough, the common pale purple form remains the most popular even though there are purple, deep blue, pink, white, and even double forms. All possess the delicious fragrance we all love.

Lilacs thrive and grow with little attention from us. Plant them in a sunny place where they'll have room to reach their ultimate height. After blooming you may wish to cut off the dried flowerheads to tidy up the shrubs' appearance. Very old shrubs (that you'll sometimes find in old neighborhoods) may have become misshapen and lost their vigor. You can rejuvenate them by the radical method of cutting them all the way to the ground in spring. They will quickly resprout and bloom in just a few years. One of the most fragrant varieties the so-called dwarf 'Miss Kim', growing to about 5' by 5' with lavender-pink blossoms that perfume your entire garden.

Potential problems: scale sometimes will attack the bark. Treat with a dormant oil spray in spring before the shrubs leaf out. Late frosts can ruin the flower display.

Lilac (*Syringa vulgaris*) with ajuga and lamb's ears.

Variegated yucca (*Yucca filamentosa* 'Variegata') with lamb's ears.

## YUCCA
### *Yucca glauca*
### Category: sun
### Use: xeriscaping, slopes, borders
### Soil: adaptable, well-drained
### Hardiness: zones 4 to 8
### Mature size: up to 5' by 2'

The toughest and most fierce wildflower in our region, yucca makes a statement. Mainly it says, "back off." Gardeners treat it with respect. Our native yucca is blue-green in color and eventually grows several feet tall with colonies of smaller plants springing up from runners near its base, resembling a family of porcupines. Tall spikes to 4' or 5' in height are studded in mid- to late summer with cream flowers blushed with pink. The petals appear to be cut from crepe. Pulling wild oats that sometimes sprout at its base is one of my least-favorite garden chores. It's worth it; the barbed spikes provide four seasons of interest. They're especially pretty iced with snow, but I always forget to get my camera.

Another yucca grown in this region is the variegated form of the species (*Y. filamentosa*). With its green blades streaked with yellow, it's very appealing in a border as an architectural element. It sets off lavender, yarrow, and lady's mantle to good effect. Not as drought tolerant or as cold hardy as the native, variegated yucca is also not quite as sharp. A related plant is the so-called red yucca (*Hesperaloe parviflora*), native to the Southwest. With its burgundy-red leaves with peeling fibers on the edges and coral or yellow flowers on its tall, thin flower stalks, red yucca makes an exciting addition to a dryland garden. Ice plants, California poppy, and Indian blanket further enhance its beauty.

Potential problems: leaves that blow into the plant can be a literal pain to remove.

**Purple 'Jackman's'** (*Clematis* x *Jackmanii*) **and red 'Niobe' clematis (***Clematis* **'Niobe').**

# VINES

✿

## CLEMATIS
### *Clematis* x *Jackmanii*
### Category: sun
### Use: trellises, fences
### Soil: adaptable, moist to moderately moist
### Hardiness: zones 4 to 7
### Mature size: up to 10'

Although drought remains an overriding concern in our region, indulging in a few plants that require constant moisture seems responsible, especially if they're grouped together in one small zone, and especially if they're as pretty and prolific as clematis. Jackman's clematis remains the most popular in our region for very good reason. It's easy and blooms profusely, cloaking a trellis or arbor in sumptuous deep purple flowers.

Clematis species and hybrids have a thick bible on their care, mainly concerning how to prune them. When planting Jackman's clematis, just remember the old axiom, "head in the sun, feet in the shade," and trim out the deadwood each spring. Basically, you can leave it alone except for providing even, consistent moisture throughout the season.

Another stellar vine is sweet autumn clematis (*C. paniculata*), a late bloomer with myriad small white flowers that smell of almonds and vanilla. It's a good scamperer that can disguise an ugly fence in a few seasons. It doesn't need much pruning except to keep it in bounds. Clematis looks lovely wandering up big upright junipers, which can take a bit of garlanding. If you try this, make sure your clematis gets enough moisture since junipers are greedy.

Potential problems: clematis is subject to a disease called clematis wilt (where the entire vine suddenly collapses overnight and doesn't recover). Since I've scared you, you might as well know about magnesium deficiency in clematis, signaled by yellowing, mottled leaves. Treat it with horticultural grade magnesium or with a few tablespoons of Epsom salts dissolved in water and poured at the base of the plant.

## MORNING GLORY
### *Ipomoea purpurea*
### Category: sun annual
### Use: trellises, arbors, fences
### Soil: adaptable, moist to somewhat dry
### Hardiness: annual
### Mature size: up to 12'

Sometimes the most beautiful flowers are also the easiest to grow. Morning glories deserve their name. On vigorous annual vines with heart-shaped leaves, the flowers unfurl in early morning in great numbers from August until frost, and they are glorious to see. They usually fold by early afternoon, but if clouds appear, they may stay open for a good part of the day. Drought and heat tolerant, the vines will twine up trellises, arbors, or fences and help to screen unsightly views.

To get your own line of morning glories started, buy a package of seed in spring. Soak the seeds overnight to soften the hard seed casing and poke them 1" deep in the soil with your fingers. They will germinate quickly if planted in a sunny spot after danger of frost has passed. You need only four or five plants to cloak a substantial trellis.

The most popular morning glory is 'Heavenly Blue', which produces sky blue funnel-like flowers 3" across. 'Scarlett O' Hara' blooms with rosy red flowers. Seed mixtures offer a range of colors from pink and white to blue and deep violet. Many older gardens have their own strains of mauve, purple, and blue morning glories that appear faithfully each year. I inherited these old favorites in my garden and they're quite pretty even if they don't bloom quite as big as 'Heavenly Blue'.

Potential problems: too much fertilizer will result in luxurious leaves without many flowers.

## SWEET POTATO
### *Ipomoea batatas*
### Category: sun
### Use: containers, borders, retaining walls
### Soil: moist, organically rich
### Hardiness: tropical
### Mature size: 6" tall by spreads up to 4'

When I was a boy, I plunked a sweet potato in a pot and grew it on the bookcase beneath my bedroom window. The vine made my room seem like the jungles in Robert Louis Stevenson novels. Many years later I'm reliving that tropical feeling on my patio. The current crop of sweet potatoes is more ornamental than the plain green one of my childhood. With either bronze or chartreuse leaves, they tumble out of pots and hanging baskets beautifully, as well as spilling down retaining walls or onto walks near the front of the border. The leaves can either be spade-shaped or dissected like a maple. Very thickly produced, they overlap to produce a cascade of color, both striking in itself as well as vibrant in contrast to flower colors.

ABOVE: 'Heavenly Blue' morning glory (*Ipomoea purpurea* 'Heavenly Blue') BELOW: Golden sweet potato (*Ipomoea batatas*) with fancy-leaf geranium, yellow flowering maple, and bronze perilla.

You can't grow wrong in making beautiful combinations as long as the companions you choose are equally as vigorous as the sweet potatoes.

In pots, I'd certainly suggest pairings with cannas, verbenas, ivy-leaf geraniums, cascading petunias, New Zealand flax (*Phormium tenax*), flowering maples (*Abutilon*), and coleus. Perhaps one of the most eye-popping containers I've seen was a luscious combo of golden sweet potato vine, black-eyed Susan, purple verbena, and orange coleus. I'm going to copy it. You should too. The bronze-leaf forms such as 'Blackie' and 'Ace of Spades' invite subtler combinations as will coral or salmon-pink twinspur (*Diascia*), fancy-leaf geraniums with contrasting bronze bands on the foliage, patio-type dahlias, and warm-toned zinnias.

Potential problems: heat and moisture encourage rampant growth (that's a good thing); a few insects will want to sample the leaves but are generally not a problem.

A trouble-free garden starts in spring with golden *Tulipa tarda* emerging through a sea of 'Betty Blake' phlox.

# ■ Troubleshooting in the Garden

It's joy to garden in the Rocky Mountain West. Compared to other regions of the country—and even the rest of the planet—this is a darned fine place to till the soil and make things grow. We often think if we just lived somewhere else, where you can stick a broomstick in the ground and it will sprout, that gardening would be so much easier. Maybe some aspects of growing would become easier, but there are always trade-offs. For instance, with more rain come more slugs and higher humidity, which breeds more fungus and disease (and more bad hair days). With more heat comes, well . . . more heat. Even in mild climates where snow never threatens, there are drawbacks, for without a cold winter there can be no tulips and lilacs.

As you begin your first garden, every little problem may seem like a big deal. Don't be discouraged; you'll quickly learn how to modify what you do to cope with the challenges that nature tosses at you. After all, everything that happens in your garden is just nature at work. Sometimes this matches your plans and sometimes it doesn't. The only troubles that may arise that aren't part of nature's design are those caused by other humans, such as a husband who gets carried away with the weed whacker, or very strange people who dig plants out of your garden. This has happened to me several times, from the woman who raided my vegetable garden and claimed she thought it was a community garden, to the villain in the night who swiped the rare penstemon seedlings I'd just set out that afternoon, to the woman I caught red-handed digging dianthus and iris in my front garden. But that's beside the point. Most gardening "problems" are really just nature taking its course. You can affect the final outcome by doing the right things at the right times.

# WISE WEED WORDS

Let's start with weeds. The worst ones in our region were here long before any of us. Puncture vine, that flat annual creeper with sharp seedpods that can flatten a bicycle tire, entered our region with Spanish explorers, perhaps in grain or stuck to the hair of animals. Thistle, tumbleweeds, and bindweed hitchhiked in with agricultural crops. Woolly mullein (*Verbascum thapsus*), related to ornamental silver mullein (*V. bombyciferum*), was planted in mining towns. The tall flower stalks were dipped in tallow and used as torches, hence the common name "miner's candle." When the mines closed and the stalks didn't get picked, the plants got out of hand.

Some plants were planted in the past as ornamentals and, without the competition and pests that keep them under control in their native habitats, have become noxious weeds. Tamarix has attached itself to our river and stream banks like a leech, sucking them dry and crowding out native vegetation. Birds spread the seeds of Russian olive into the wild. The herb tansy now grows all too luxuriantly in the Roaring Fork Valley of Colorado. And I don't have to tell even a beginner about dandelions, perhaps the worst import ever from England.

Even seemingly demure garden perennials sometimes display a Jeckyll-and-Hyde personality. Some of the most aggressive include ribbon grass, 'Valerie Finnis' artemisia, snow-on-the-mountain (sometimes called bishop's weed), buttercups, and sweet woodruff. This doesn't mean that these plants should not be considered for your garden, especially in really tough spots where very little else wants to grow, such as dry shade. A friend of mine who gardens in a shady city lot uses them to good advantage since they can almost keep up with the digging tendencies of her Russian wolfhound. (She claims "borzoi" is Russian for "backhoe," but we'll talk more about pets shortly.) These plants can be useful when you're aware of what they can do and, to my knowledge, have not escaped into the wild. Three other thugs really should be on the permanent "do not grow" list—bell flower (*Campanula rapunculoides*), fleece flower or mile-a-minute-plant (that should tip you off) (*Polygonum aubertii*), and ground ivy (*Glechoma hederacea*). They're pretty much unstoppable and without merit, except for the bellflower. It's a pretty thing with thin stems to 2' or 3' tall with lavender-blue bells, but it's been known to devour entire neighborhoods. Don't accept a clump of it from a friend who's actually desperately trying to clear his own yard of it.

This all sounds terrible, perhaps scaring you off before you even start. It's not so bad. You may face few of these weeds if you move into an established, well-maintained landscaped new home. If you're starting from scratch—on "virgin" ground—you'll likely encounter mainly native plants (and don't decide they're weeds just because they're wild). Foreign weeds, in general, thrive in disturbed soil. That's why you see them along roadsides, train tracks, and vacant lots. That's also why you'll get them in your own plot when you begin to disturb the soil. Nature looks for opportunities, and it's your job to re-plant and cover the soil with plants of your choice before that soil blows away and before nature does your re-planting for you with plants not of your preference.

Don't be fooled by gimmicks that promise weed-free gardens. The only way to get a weed-free garden is to weed it. Tackle weeds when they're small, rather than wrestling with giants. Get them before they go to seed, or your problem will multiply a hundredfold next year. Go after the worst thugs, such as thistle and bindweed, with the big guns. Carefully and methodically apply a non-selective weed killer, or smother them for a year under black plastic or thick layers of newspaper. Or both. Get aggressive, solve the problem, and your densely planted new garden will likely have few weed problems you can't handle from then on.

## THE FOOD CHAIN

Most animals eat plants. They have no idea that the plants in your garden are exclusively yours. You paid for them and lovingly planted them, but slugs, caterpillars, rabbits, and deer did not get the e-mail regarding your territorial rights. You'll need to enforce them. Fencing is about the only truly effective way to keep out deer, elk, and rabbits. Yes, some plants are relatively unpalatable to these critters. And yes, some people get good results with deterrents, including pepper sprays, soap, mothballs, blood meal, sirens, and heavy-metal rock. I think a "for sale" sign would appear in my front yard if my neighbors used such tactics.

Animal populations go through cycles and are affected by weather and predators. Many gardeners in my city noticed an explosion in the rabbit population this past year. It turns out there's been a concerted effort to remove coyotes and foxes because of their perceived threat to pets and children. For every action there's a reaction. My neighborhood coexists with foxes and all I can say is that rabbits and mice are rare. My dogs, who stay inside at night, sometimes run to the French doors in my bedroom overlooking the garden and go ballistic when they sense the intrusion of other critters. I think the foxes are about (or maybe burglars). Either way, it's good to have alert, noisy dogs. Wherever you live, animals live nearby and some might eat your plants or eat the animals that eat your plants. Your local garden center or county extension agent can offer you options to deal with ground squirrels, voles, rabbits, mice, squirrels, raccoons, snakes, and so forth. I have a friend who gardens in the mountains. She always checks her property for bears before she goes out to putter. That puts our minor critter encounters in perspective.

## A BUG'S LIFE

Some of the most troublesome animals are the tiniest. Insects cause more stress than they really should. As I've explained earlier, my best advice for dealing with bugs is to take natural approaches to control and to strive to create a healthy ecosystem. If you wake up early on a beautiful summer day and you go out into your garden, you'll know if you succeeded. Spider webs will glisten with dew throughout your plantings, ready to snare whiteflies and fungus gnats. Ladybugs will be perched on roses and columbines, feasting on aphids. The goldfish in your pond will be searching for mosquito larvae. Bees will start buzzing around your flowers and vegetables to ensure pollination. Birds will drink and bathe in the water you've provided, ready to gobble down grubs and caterpillars. Bats may just be roosting after their night patrol for flying insects. You can turn over the grapefruit halves you put out yesterday and squish the slugs underneath—just to get the day off to a good start. I'm not being silly, this happens to me nearly every morning.

Healthy, non-stressed plants most easily withstand insects and disease. Speaking of disease, there are so few serious ones that attack plants in our region that I'm having trouble thinking of them. There's mildew, of course, but it's hardly life-threatening, and there are various rusts that attack hollyhocks, mountain ash, and a few other plants.

Sometimes you might encounter an anomaly that disrupts your little paradise. It could be a plague of grasshoppers or an attack of earwigs. Your lilacs may get scale (flat insects that attach to the bark and suck the sap). Or a drought-stressed blue spruce or pine may fall victim to beetles. These need immediate attention by a trained arborist as soon as you notice a problem. Despite my aversion to chemical sprays, it may be necessary to use them in order save a tree. Usually there's an underlying problem such as old age, poor drainage, or drought that has made the tree vulnerable to other damage by insects or disease. After the arborist treats the obvious problem, attempt to determine a long-term solution—although with some older trees you may just be prolonging the inevitable.

One common problem that you can help solve yourself is leaf scorch on deciduous trees. In this condition, it appears as if the leaf has been blow-torched, with the outside fringes all brown and green remaining only on the inside. What's happened is that the tree, optimistic in spring, has determined that it doesn't have enough water to keep everything going during the heat. It sacrifices the outer part of the leaf to save the interior part so it can keep photosynthesis going. You can't reverse this condition but, with deep watering, you can help the tree through the rest of the season so it doesn't go into winter in a dry, vulnerable state. Most spring tree loss is the result of poor conditions the trees have endured over several previous summers. I sometimes act as a guest on radio shows where people can call in with their gardening questions. A woman once called in June saying that one of her trees had not yet leafed out. I tried to explain that several years of drought had taken its toll. She refused to accept this and argued with me for quite some time. Finally I declared, "Madam, your tree is dead!" and hung up.

## WHO LET THE DOGS IN?

If you asked my dogs on any given day how their day had been, I suspect they'd all say it was the best day ever. On a typical day, they got to play in the garden, chased squirrels, looked for mice under the porch, and barked at the neighbor's motorcycle. Some might assume dogs and a beautiful garden cannot coexist. That's not so. You just might need to lower your standards a bit. Paths have been created where I never intended them. Flats of annuals sitting on the patio, ready for tomorrow's planting, make excellent toys, first to be pulled from their pots, then for the fun of chewing the plastic. Patio pots are obviously there to be jumped over or to be looped as tightly as possible—at the fastest pace possible. With some training, Gruff would make a great barrel racer. Each summer a few pots mysteriously get broken.

Some people would stress over such rambunctious behavior and consign the dogs to a run. But what's the point of having dogs if you keep them cooped up instead of with you? I like it when Gruff, Katie, and Rose hang out with me while I garden, even if I spend too much time

**Squirrel chasers have no respect for plants, so when Rose gets too wild,
I can close the gate between the patio and garden.**

persuading them not to sit on the plants (I have two cats as well, but they live indoors where only the palms and asparagus ferns are at peril). Gardening is pretty much a foreign concept to dogs, except for the digging part. As I planted clumps of hen and chicks along a path last summer, Rose (a cattle dog–Labrador mix) stayed faithfully at my side. When I looked back at the ten feet I'd just planted, I discovered Rose had systematically un-planted each one the moment I'd moved on. But we're definitely on the same wavelength when it comes to planting bulbs. This looks perfectly reasonable to them; the urge to bury food is strong with my dogs, especially the two Scottish terriers. Even in winter, when the soil is frozen, I find Milk Bones hidden under pillows, piles of dirty laundry and, of course, in potted plants. None of this is new to other pet owners, who probably check carefully before they throw clothes in the washing machine, too.

Gardening (and living) with pets has required me to make adjustments. This is a good thing, since my past obsessive-compulsive approach wore me out. I'm glad to have an excuse for lowering my housekeeping standards. This is best illustrated by my "no pets on the furniture" rule, which collapsed after about three days. All that remains of that dictum is "no pets under the covers"—except, of course, during thunderstorms. This is starting to sound a lot like *The Sound of Music*—with me playing governess to an all-animal cast. Next thing you know, I'll be making play clothes for my dogs from my bedroom curtains. Which brings me to discussion of a play area.

My dogs pretty much have the run of the garden, but I can close the gate separating the patio and the main borders. That way, they can't just tear through it at a dead run when they go defend their territory against dogs being walked down the sidewalk. But along the side of the house that faces the street and behind, along the alley, they have free reign. This shady, cool no-gardener's-land is littered with toys and socks (and holes) amongst a few sturdy shrubs and ground covers. I guess it is a dog run—they certainly do a lot of running in it.

Some plants can take more punishment than others. Brittle tulips, begonias, impatiens, and dahlias should be kept out of harm's way. Most perennials and ornamental grasses—the bigger the better—can withstand some romping, along with ground covers such as creeping verbenas, thyme, coral bells, lady's mantle, vinca, and creeping phlox. My dogs have never taken the slightest interest in eating any plants from the garden, except grass. They seem to need that canine equivalent of a spring tonic, which they usually deposit in another form on the living room rug. Cats like grass, too, so my solution is to keep pots of easily sprouted oat grass going most of the year so everybody can get their fill. If you're worried about pets or toddlers ingesting poisonous plants, avoid growing daffodils, lily-of-the-valley, castor beans, foxglove, and many others that you can check about with your garden center.

Beds and borders can also be framed with a short hedge to create a dense wall. It has to be "unhoppable," so the height would depend on your dog's agility. I've considered a barberry or privet hedge running along the fronts of my borders, giving them a neat "picture frame" effect. And then I envision the dogs following me as I clip the hedges, shaking their heads in bewilderment over how silly humans can be.

# Resources

## NURSERIES

**A Korner Flower Mart**
3424 Dillon Dr.
Pueblo, CO 81003
719-585-0287

**Birdsall & Co**
1540 S. Broadway
Denver, CO 80210-2608
303-722-2535

**Cashel Farms Nurseries**
14850 Holtwood Rd.
Simla, CO 80835
719-541-2417

**City Floral**
1440 Kearney St.
Denver, CO 80220
303-399-1177

**Echter's Greenhouse
& Gardens**
5150 Garrison St.
Arvada, CO 80002-4246
303-424-7979

**Fort Collins Nursery**
2121 E. Mulberry St.
Fort Collins, CO 80524-3696
970-482-1984

**Grand Junction Nursery Garden**
2862 North Ave.
Grand Junction, CO 81501-5011
970-242-5528

**High Country Gardens Inc.**
2930 Hwy. 92
Hotchkiss, CO 81419-9544
970-872-4402

**Los Robles Nursery Co.**
918 W. Costilla St.
Colorado Springs, CO 80905-1779
719-636-3258

**Pagosa Nursery Co.**
166 Bastille Dr.
Pagosa Springs, CO 81147-9388
970-731-4126

**Rabbit Shadow Farm**
2880 E. State Hwy. 402
Loveland, CO 80537
970-667-5531

**The Tree Farm**
11868 Mineral Rd.,
Longmont, CO 80504
303-652-2961

**Blooms Blossoms & Blisters**
720 S. Challis St.
Salmon, ID 83467-4735
208-756-6045

**Cloverdale Nursery**
2528 N. Cloverdale Rd.
Boise, ID 83713-4999
208-375-5262

**Fiddler's Ridge Farm**
1001 Fiddlers Ridge Loop
Potlatch, ID 83855-8724
208-875-1003

**High Mountain Nursery**
203 N. 3rd St.
McCall, ID 83638-5020
208-634-7228

**Pocatello Greenhouse**
1300 E. Oak St.
Pocatello, ID 83201-3261
208-232-7985

**Sun Valley Garden Center**
771 N. Main St.
Bellevue, ID 83313-5081
208-788-3533

**Wintergreen Gardens**
319 W. Beech St.
Caldwell, ID 83605-5668
208-454-8031

**Big Sky Nursery & Greenhouse**
1500 E. Railroad St.
Laurel, MT 59044-3340
406-628-6827

**Billings Nursery**
2147 Poly Dr.
Billings, MT 59102-1654
406-656-5501

**Bitterroot Nursery**
521 Eastside Hwy.
Hamilton, MT 59840-9225
406-961-3806

**Cut Bank Greenhouse**
421 First St. N.W.
Cut Bank, MT 59427-2607
406-873-2243

**Heartsong Gardens**
5364 Eastside Hwy.
Stevensville, MT 59870-6354
406-777-7163

**Pink Grizzly**
1400 Wyoming St.
Missoula, MT 59801-1724
406-728-3370

**Wild Geese Gardens**
1403 Fourth St. W.
Kalispell, MT 59901-4224
406-755-3744

**Country Gardens Floral**
106 Business Loop W.
Jamestown, ND 58401-5243
701-251-2030

**Elm River Garden Center**
Highway 81 N.
Grandin, ND 58038
701-484-5591

**Handy Andy's Drive Inn Nursery**
Highway 2 W.
Williston, ND 58801
701-572-6083

**Prairie Wood Nursery**
600 Twelfth St. N.E.
Watford City, ND 58854
701-842-6348

**Wildrose Nursery**
2202 Sixth Ave. E.
Williston, ND 58801-6242
701-572-7915

**Dakota Greenhouse**
815 E. Seventh St.
Dell Rapids, SD 57022-1736
605-428-3929

**Homestead Nursery**
S. Hwy. 85
Belle Fourche, SD 57717
605-892-2846

**Madison Nursery & Landscape**
215 S.E. Tenth St.
Madison, SD 57042-3402
605-256-4112

**Whetstone Valley Greenhouse**
RR 1 Box 183
Sisseton, SD 57262-9104
605-698-3617

**Yankton Nurseries LLC**
2000 Ferdig St.
Yankton, SD 57078-1860
605-665-6560

**Ballard's Nursery**
691 N. State St.
Hurricane, UT 84737-1776
435-635-4274

**Beaver Nursery**
640 S. Main St., P.O. Box 2300
Beaver, UT 84713
435-438-2254

**Canyon Breeze Garden Nursery**
551 N. 300 E.
Parowan, UT 84761
435-477-8007

**Great Basin Native**
75 W. 300 S.
Holden, UT 84636
435-795-2303

**High Desert Gardens**
2971 S. Hwy. 191
Moab, UT 84532-3438
435-259-4531

**Intermountain Nursery**
340 W. Bastian Lane
Sigurd, UT 84657
435-896-8100

**Marmalade Hill Nursery**
5889 S. 4950 W.
Hooper, UT 84315-9512
801-985-2359

**Park City Nursery**
4497 Hwy. 224
Park City, UT 84098-5977
435-649-1363

**Sunshine Greenhouses**
384 S. 3110 W.
Provo, UT 84601-3632
801-377-2477

**Western Garden Center (SLC store)**
550 S. 600 E.
Salt Lake City, UT 84102-2795
801-364-7871

**Aspen Grove Nursery**
43 Aspen Grove Dr.
Evanston, WY 82930
307-789-2775

**Cody Greenhouses**
3279 Big Horn Ave.
Cody, WY 82414-9250
307-527-6418

**Little Goose Native Plants**
226 Main St.
Big Horn, WY 82833
307-672-5340

**Rawlins Doggett Greenhouse**
504 23rd St.
Rawlins, WY 82301-5154
307-324-2434

**Western Nursery
& Landscaping**
12950 Shinn Rd.
Casper, WY 82604-9592
307-265-0193

## MAIL-ORDER SUPPLIERS

**Laporte Avenue Nursery**
1950 Laporte Ave.
Fort Collins, CO 80521
970-472-0017
*Alpine and rock garden plants.*

**Old House Gardens**
536 Third St.
Ann Arbor, MI 48103-4957
734-995-1486; Fax 734-995-1687
www.oldhousegardens.com
*Heirloom bulbs, including spring-blooming tulips, daffodils, crocus and hyacinths and summer-blooming dahlias, cannas, and gladiolus.*

**J. W. Jung Seed Company**
335 S. High St.
Randolph, WI 53957-0001
800-297-3123; Fax 800-692-5864
www.jungseed.com
*Perennials, roses, shrubs, vegetable and annual seeds.*

**Fantasy Orchids, Inc.**
830 W. Cherry St.
Louisville, CO 80027
303-666-5432
www.fantasyorchids.com
*Huge selection of orchids.*

**Nichols Garden Nursery**
1190 Old Salem Rd. N.E.
Albany, OR 97321-4580
800-422-3985
www.nicholsgardennursery.com
*Herb plants, seeds of herbs, annuals, vegetables.*

**Botanical Interests**
660 Compton St.
Broomfield, CO 80020
800.486.2647
www.botanicalinterests.com
*On-line seed merchants with wide selection of wild flower, perennial, annual, and vegetable seed.*

**High Country Gardens**
2902 Rufina St.
Santa Fe, NM 87507
800-925-9387; Fax 800-925-0097
www.highcountrygardens.com
*Native and adaptable perennials.*

**Renee's Garden**
7389 W. Zayante Rd.
Felton, CA 95018
888-880-7228
www.reneesgarden.com
*Cottage garden flowers, herbs, and gourmet vegetable seeds.*

**The Fragrant Path**
P.O. Box 328
Ft. Calhoun, NE 68023
*Seeds of fragrant annuals, perennials, and vines.*

## EXTENSION SERVICES

State University Cooperative Extension Service web sites:
http://www.ext.colostate.edu/ (Colorado)
http://www.uidaho.edu/ag/extension/ (Idaho)
http://extension.usu.edu/cooperative/ (Utah)
http://uwadmnweb.uwyo.edu/UWces/ (Wyoming)
http://www.ext.nodak.edu/ (North Dakota)
http://www3.sdstate.edu/CooperativeExtension/ (South Dakota)
http://extn.msu.montana.edu/ (Montana)

## SUGGESTED READING

Busco, Janice, and Nancy R. Morin. *Native Plants for High-Elevation Western Gardens* (Fulcrum Publishing, 2003).

Denver Water, *Xeriscape Plant Guide: 100 Water-Wise Plants for Gardens and Landscapes* (Fulcrum Publishing, 1998).

Proctor, Rob, and David Macke, *Herbs in the Garden: The Art of Intermingling* (Interweave Press, 1997).

Raff, Marilyn, *The Intuitive Gardener: Finding Creative Freedom in the Garden* (Fulcrum Publishing, 2003).

Springer, Lauren, *The Undaunted Garden: Planting for Weather-Resilient Beauty* (Fulcrum Publishing, 1997).

Springer, Lauren, and Rob Proctor. *Passionate Gardening: Good Advice for Challenging Climates* (Fulcrum Publishing, 2000).

Tweit, Susan, *Rocky Mountain Garden Survival Guide* (Fulcrum Publishing, 2004).

# Index

**NOTE: page numbers in italics indicate illustrations.**